A GUIDE TO JEWISH PRACTICE

THE
JOURNEY
OF *MOURNING*

A GUIDE
to JEWISH
PRACTICE

Center for Jewish Ethics
Reconstructionist Rabbinical College
in cooperation with the
Reconstructionist Rabbinical Association

Reconstructionist Rabbinical College Press

1299 Church Road, Wyncote, PA 19095-1898
www.rrc.edu

THE *JOURNEY* OF *MOURNING*

RICHARD HIRSH

Dedication

The Journey of Mourning is dedicated with appreciation to the members of the congregations I have had the opportunity to serve as rabbi. By allowing me into their lives at moments of loss, they showed me the many ways in which Jewish tradition could be a source of comfort, of strength and of wisdom in confronting death. This book is for them, and for all who travel the path of the journey of mourning.

Richard Hirsh

Reconstructionist Rabbinical College Press
Wyncote, Pennsylvania

Composition by G&H Soho, Inc.

ISBN 0-938945-10-6

2005935343

Printed in the U.S.A.

Contents

Commentators

Daniel Goldman Cedarbaum (D.G.C.)

Dan Ehrenkrantz (D.E.)

Dayle A. Friedman (D.A.F.)

Richard Hirsh (R.H.)

Myriam Klotz (M.K.)

Barbara Rosman Penzner (B.R.P.)

Linda Potemken (L.P.)

Simcha Raphael (S.R.)

Yael Ridberg (Y.R.)

Brant Rosen (B.R.)

Sheila Peltz Weinberg (S.P.W.)

David Zinner (D.Z.)

Advisory Committee

Rabbis Richard Hirsh and David Teutsch, *Co-chairs*

Rabbi Lester Bronstein

Chayim Herzig-Marx

Leah Kamionkowski

Dr. Tamar Kamionkowski

Rabbi Nina Mandel

Rabbi Yael Ridberg

Rabbi Jacob Staub

Preface

This edition of *The Journey of Mourning* is one chapter from what will eventually be a full volume entitled *A Guide to Jewish Practice: The Life-Cycle*. It is presented here as an independent volume in response to requests from rabbis, mourners, educators and others who have used previous editions and asked that we continue to make this material available in this format.

Earlier versions appeared as a pamphlet published by the Reconstructionist Rabbinical Association (2001); in *Kol Haneshamah:Prayers for a House of Mourning* (The Reconstructionist Press, 2001); and in *Beḥoref Hayamim, In the Winter of Life* (Reconstructionist Rabbinical College Center for Jewish Ethics, 2002). Rabbi David Teutsch originally invited me to write *The Journey of Mourning* for inclusion in *Kol Haneshamah: Prayers for a House of Mourning*. I thank him for that opportunity and for his guidance, input and suggestions that have helped to shape this expanded version.

The commentators who have enriched the text with their contributions gave generously of their time, responded promptly to editorial suggestions, and waited patiently for the publication of this volume. I am grateful for their participation in this project; their wise words have enriched the text.

Both the former and current executive assistants at the Reconstructionist Rabbinical Association, Linda Kaplan and Sharon Presser, helped prepare the manuscript, and I thank each of them for their support. Cheryl Plumly stepped in as the manuscript was almost finished to provide essential technical support, and I thank her for her good will and good work. Marilyn Silverstein provided expert copy-editing as well as many helpful suggestions that improved the text. Leah Kamionkowski contributed to the integrity of this volume with her helpful comments and suggestions. Dr. Simcha Raphael and David Zinner contributed to clarifications and corrections that appear in this edition.

The Jewish Reconstructionist Federation kindly gave permission to use selections from the *Kol Haneshamah* prayer-book series, including Joel Rosenberg's translations of the *El Maley Raḥamim* prayer and the Kaddish.

Finally, my thanks to the Reconstructionist Rabbinical College's Center for Jewish Ethics and its director, David Teutsch, for undertaking the publication of this volume.

Richard Hirsh
December 2005 / Hanukka 5766

THE
JOURNEY
OF MOURNING

Introduction

Few moments in human life carry as much meaning as those that touch on the boundaries of life. Jewish rituals and observances can help guide us through such moments. Traditions, values and customs can help create meaning and structure as well as provide comfort at times of transition.

Life's boundary moments can be disruptive and disturbing, and the death of a loved one in particular can be destabilizing. Death makes us aware of the inevitable and universal transience of life, and alongside our sorrow we hear the echo of our own mortality that accompanies moments of grieving and memorializing.

The purpose of this guide is to suggest basic Reconstructionist practices that can serve as spiritual resources for mourners and for those who comfort mourners. A guide is not a code; it does not prescribe what each individual should do. A guide is a pathway through Jewish tradition that provides explanations, illuminates values and suggests approaches that are responsive to the needs of contemporary Jews.

A Reconstructionist guide reflects two fundamental commitments:

> » *Fidelity* to the customs and traditions of the Jewish people, for each generation of Jews is the custodian

of Judaism and bears the responsibility of ensuring its preservation and transmission.

» *Responsiveness* to the needs of contemporary Jews, reflected in a willingness to adapt and innovate.

From a traditional as well as a contemporary perspective, many Jewish practices associated with mourning are subject to adaptation and to the customs of different communities. What may be standard in one locale would not necessarily be done elsewhere. While the decision regarding which rituals and customs to observe is the responsibility of each mourner, a rabbi can help provide information and insight as to what is essential and what is marginal, what is recommended and what is discouraged. A rabbi can also help identify the general patterns of observance within a community as a way of providing communal guidance to individual mourners.

Explanations for rituals vary widely. Traditions surrounding death and mourning are in many cases centuries old, and the origins of customs are usually obscure, although some explanations are accepted as normative. Reconstructionism affirms the possibility of reading new meanings into old rituals while preserving those rituals out of a sense of continuity and commitment.

Decisions about which funeral and burial traditions to observe are the responsibility of the mourner, but practices and policies of the congregation, the community, the rabbi, the funeral director, the cemetery, the *ḥevra ḳadisha* and others will need to be taken into account. — D.Z.

Because death is so profoundly disorienting, we are often eager to make use of as much of our tradition as possible to help us cope with loss. Previous patterns of personal and/or family ritual observance may be minimal, but mourners often seek to comply with maximal mourning practice. Certainly, more Jewish observance can help mourners find comfort and consolation, and from a Reconstructionist perspective, few particular practices are discouraged. But mourners should be cautious about trying to fulfill every custom conveyed to them by well-meaning friends and relatives as well as by traditional codes of Jewish law. It is easy to be overwhelmed by a sense of obligation and a need to "do the right thing." In a quest for precision, it is possible to miss the opportunity for Jewish tradition to serve the spiritual and emotional needs of mourners.

Throughout this guide, the words *mitzva* and *mitzvot* are used to refer to the observances of tradition that contemporary Jews should consider seriously as practices for themselves. These traditions are rooted in the experiences of generations of the Jewish people, and come to us as imperatives based on the wisdom, sanctity and meaning they embody.

Making reasoned and well-considered decisions at a time of loss is difficult. Tradition can serve as a valuable guide. Yet if we heed the voice of tradition without question, trying to observe all laws and customs, what might have been comforting and helpful can become demanding and confusing. If we can study Jewish laws and customs before facing a loss, we will have a better perspective from which to sift the tradition for what may be helpful. — D.E.

Jewish tradition focuses on three primary *mitzvot* at the time of death:

» ***Mitzvot*** **of *Avelut*/Mourning:** This refers to the *obligations/opportunities for mourners* in terms of traditions and customs they observe as part of their mourning. From the rich patterns of observance marking the journey through mourning and back into life, mourners should select those rituals and rites that help support them and lend stability during a time that often appears without structure.

» ***Mitzvot*** **of *K'vod Hamet*/Honoring the Deceased.** This refers to *obligations to the deceased person,* including the care extended to the body between death and burial and the norm of a dignified and respectful interment shortly after death.

» ***Mitzvot*** **of *Niḥum Avelim*/Comforting the Mourners:** This refers to the *obligation of friends and family* to support and comfort the mourners. There are rituals and customs pertaining to comforters as well as to those in need of comfort.

For each stage of the journey of mourning, this guide describes *mitzvot* associated with these categories. Discussions of such broader topics as who is a mourner, the Kad-

---

Reconstructionist practice works toward a balance between the traditional and the innovative, between communal needs and individual needs. Rather than encouraging mourners to pick and choose, we should help them understand the cohesive pattern of Jewish death and mourning practices, and help them make meaningful choices. — D.Z.

dish, cremation, funerals, Shiva and Jewish holidays, infant death, and suggestions for interfaith and conversionary family circumstances are found beginning on page 50.

In view of traditional Jewish strictures against cremation and prevailing contemporary sentiment in favor of burial, throughout this guide "burial" is used as the normal referent for the final disposition of the body. An extended discussion of issues and options with regard to the choice of cremation is on page 57.

Aninut: *From Death to Burial*

The period from death to burial is one of intense emotion and personal and family disruption. Mourners are involved with making arrangements for the funeral and burial and notifying family and friends.

***Mitzvot* of *Avelut*/Mourning:** One becomes a mourner upon hearing of a death. The period from the time one receives the news of a death until the burial is called *aninut*, derived from a Hebrew word meaning "impoverished" or "afflicted"—which accurately captures the intensity of the first stage in the journey of mourning. (Who is a "mourner"? See page 50.)

Aninut is a particularly difficult period. The often shattering news of a loss can be numbing, and yet the inevitable task of beginning to accept the death also claims attention. The necessity of making funeral and burial arrangements often supersedes the need to express the intense and complex emotions that are present.

Upon hearing of the death, mourners recite the *b'rakha* (benediction), "*Barukh Ata Adonai Eloheynu Melekh*

The first response to a death is often denial, an emotional shield that allows us to acknowledge the loss without yet feeling its full impact. This can serve a valuable function: Funeral and Shiva observances often require extensive planning, and *aninut* is when these arrangements often must be made. The denial that often accompanies this phase of mourning can help us to be more effective in carrying out the necessary tasks that precede a funeral.   — D.E.

Ha'olam, Dayan Ha'emet, Blessed are you, Wise One our God, sovereign of all worlds, the true judge."

This ancient benediction reflects our ancestors' belief that all that happens in our world is in some way the will of God, and therefore even sad news should be acknowledged by affirming God and God's decrees. Reconstructionist Judaism retains the traditional words of the Hebrew blessing as one way of wrapping mourners in the comforting rituals of Judaism. However, as we understand God more as a Power operating in and through us than as a Person acting upon us, what we mean by this benediction is something like, "We affirm the blessings of life even as we accept the boundaries of life."

After saying this *b'rakha,* one rends a garment as a sign of grieving. This is called *k'ria* (tearing). A black ribbon often substitutes for an actual garment, and is similarly torn or cut. In many communities this is deferred until the funeral service, but need not be. The garment or ribbon is worn

Saying the shortened version of the traditional prayer ("*Barukh Dayan Ha'emet*" "Blessed be the One who judges in truth") is an affirmation that there is meaning and purpose in life *and* in death, even if they are not always apparent to us in the moment. — S.R.

How do we go on living when we lose those we love? What is life worth if death is the end? Responding to death by affirming God is an attempt to keep us from despair. Although we may not be able to match our emotions to the words, the *b'rakha,* "Barukh Dayan Ha'emet," and the Mourner's Kaddish compel us to give voice to an affirmation of God and of life. We hope that the words we offer and our experience of life will eventually be reunited. — D.E.

How ironic that many modern Jews—who are often wealthier and have larger wardrobes than their ancestors might ever have imagined—almost uniformly substitute a black ribbon for an actual garment in observance of *k'ria.* Are we simply afraid (almost literally) to bare our emotional scars? — D.G.C.

through the end of the Shiva observance except on Shabbat. The tear should be on the right side of the garment, or the ribbon should be worn on the right side of the chest, except when mourning a parent, when the tear should be on the left, closer to the heart.

During *aninut*, mourners alter their patterns of living in response to the change in their lives brought about by a death and in anticipation of the observances of Shiva that commence following the burial. It is customary during *aninut* for mourners to abstain from meat and wine, symbols of enrichment; it is appropriate to withdraw from

Traditionally, the rending of a garment was done immediately upon hearing of a death. While *k'ria* is now more often done just prior to the funeral service, mourners can use that moment to make a connection to when they first learned of their loss.   — Y.R.

K'ria might be understood as symbolic of an inner spiritual wounding that occurs with the loss of a loved one. Wounds are painful. They mark us indelibly, and transform us in ways both seen and unseen, yet wounds can also heal. If we participate actively in the healing process, the pain of loss often diminishes over time. Through *k'ria*, we bear witness both to our present pain and to our eventual healing.
— B.R.

The rabbi or funeral director will usually ask for the deceased's "Hebrew name." (This might be a Yiddish or Ladino name, not necessarily a "Hebrew" one.) This name will be used in the memorial prayer *El Maley Raḥamim* ("God, overflowing with compassion . . .") and later will often be preserved on the grave marker. One's full Hebrew name includes the name of one's parents (e.g., *Leah bat Yosef v'Sara,* Leah the daughter of Joseph and Sarah). Finding the Hebrew names of the parents of the deceased may require some investigation among relatives. Such names can be found recorded on a *ketuba* (Jewish marriage certificate), if one can still be traced in a family. The process of finding these names can lead to a deeper understanding of the history of the family.   — B.R.P.

Besides funeral preparations, there are no prescribed rituals for *aninut.* One funeral director I worked with would give families a *yahrtzeit* candle to take home after making funeral arrangements. He would encourage them to light it on the afternoon or evening before the funeral and then replace it with the seven-day Shiva

one's work, both domestic and professional; one avoids entertainment, such as movies, shows and concerts.

Jewish tradition urges that burial occur as soon as possible after death. With due time allowed for family notification and necessary travel, funerals normally occur within one to three days following a death; hence, the duration of *aninut* is relatively short.

Mitzvot of ***K'vod Hamet*/Honoring the Deceased:** Between death and burial, there is great care and concern for the body of the deceased. Arrangements should be made with the funeral director for a *shomer/shomeret* (guardian) to sit with the body so that it is not left alone. A *shomer/shomeret* normally recites from the biblical book of Psalms while in the presence of the body. The origins of this practice may reside in a belief that the body/soul was vulnerable to supernatural forces following

candle when they returned home the funeral. Having a simple ritual such as lighting a candle in the home can be a helpful spiritual aid during *aninut*.   — S.R.

There is great wisdom in the Jewish practice not to prolong the time between death and burial. *Aninut* can feel like "neither here nor there"—a loved one has died, and we are suspended in time. We need to allow the waves of grief and the rites of mourning to commence, so that we might feel the warm embrace of family and community in the absence of the embrace of the deceased.   — Y.R.

Serving as a *shomer/shomeret* for a dear friend or for the loved one of a community member can be seen as both a privilege and an honor. Congregations can benefit by creating a roster of on-call *shomrim,* dramatically emphasizing the mutual interdependence of community members.   — B.R.P.

Communities can be encouraged to set up a schedule for different people to sit *shmira* for and with the deceased; two- or three-hour assignments work well and allow for more people to participate. As friends, family and community members stay with the body and recite psalms, they become part of the communal mourning process.   — S.R.

death but before interment. This practice may also derive from ancient pragmatic practices designed to protect the body from animals and insects prior to burial. Today, having a *shomer/shomeret* is recognized as a sign of respect for the deceased.

Families should ascertain whether the deceased left instructions regarding organ donation. While Judaism has traditionally placed restrictions on organ donation (as well as on routine autopsies) as a violation of *k'vod hamet,* Reconstructionist Judaism affirms that medical benefits to the living outweigh traditional restrictions against organ donation. A small number of contemporary Orthodox authorities have also ruled in favor of organ donation under certain circumstances. Where autopsies advance medical knowledge, families may choose to allow autopsies. In many communities, local laws often mandate autopsy.

Tahara (ritual purification and washing of the body) should be arranged. This is normally done by a group of volunteers known as a *hevra kadisha,* "sacred society." Today, in addition to a traditional *hevra kadisha,* a significant number of Jewish communities have a progressive/liberal *hevra kadisha.* Rabbis and/or funeral directors can

---

Every congregation can become a resource to members at a time of loss. A reminder in the monthly synagogue newsletter should list the appropriate names and information for those who are to be contacted when a death occurs. Staff and volunteers should be trained and prepared to handle these calls.   — D.Z.

In the Orthodox Jewish community, as well as in Israel, organ donation has become more common, and has earned halakhic approval from many noted rabbis.   — D.Z.

usually provide the names and contacts for local *ḥevra kadisha* organizations.

Humility and simplicity should guide the burial preparations. Commercial and consumer pressures often conspire at the moment of death, when mourners are most vulnerable and least able to think clearly. A close friend or family member can often help by accompanying mourners to the meeting with the funeral director and gently but firmly communicating the family's preference for traditional rites and rituals. Simple clothes or, according to tradition, humble burial shrouds called *takhrikhim* are used for interment: In death, all are equal. For this same reason, there is a strong preference for a plain wooden casket.

During the *tahara,* the members of the *ḥevra ḳadisha* are expected to focus their attention on preserving the *ḳavana* (intention) of honoring the deceased. The washing of the body is done with great care and sensitivity. It is customary to speak only about what is necessary for the preparation of the body. After the *tahara* concludes, and before the casket is closed, the members of the *ḥevra ḳadisha* may ask forgiveness from the deceased for anything that might have happened unintentionally during the *tahara.* — Y.R.

Burial in the land of Israel was considered meritorious. When Jacob was about to die in the land of Egypt, he made his son Joseph promise to have him buried in the land of Israel. (Genesis 49:29) Throughout much of Jewish history, burial in Israel was beyond the means of most Jews living outside of its borders. There is a tradition of placing some earth from the land of Israel inside the casket as part of the *tahara.* This may have originated as a symbolic way of enacting burial in the land of Israel. The small sample of earth from *Eretz Yisrael* becomes a tangible sign of the bond between the people Israel and the land of Israel, and of the connection between the deceased person and the Jewish people. — Y.R./R.H.

When there is a traditional *tahara,* earth specifically from the Mount of Olives in Jerusalem is sprinkled in the casket. The traditional understanding of this practice is as an affirmation of hope in the resurrection of the dead, which, according to rabbinic teachings, will begin at the Mount of Olives in the time of future redemption.
— S.R.

The tendency to overextend on funeral arrangements is often a reflex of a genuine desire to show affection and respect for the deceased. However, ostentation should be avoided. The expenses associated with elaborate arrangements—including fancy caskets and flowers—can be allocated instead to various *tzedaka* (charity) opportunities in memory of the deceased. Prior to the funeral, families should select charities to which donations may be made in memory of the deceased.

Several Reconstructionist congregations have created funeral plans that establish the community's preferred and customary rituals to be observed at a time of loss. The arrangements included in such funeral plans are then communicated to any funeral director with whom the family and rabbi may be working.

Mitzvot of *Niḥum Avelim*/Comforting the Mourners: The normal routines of life are disrupted immediately following a death. Offers to help mourners by shopping, driving a carpool, picking up relatives arriving from out of town and similar errands are all appropriate.

Friends and neighbors often want to help the bereaved. When people ask what they can do, mourners should take them up on their offer. Among the things that can be helpful: setting up the house for Shiva (provide paper goods, trash bags, beverages, guest book, a binder to keep bills and receipts and other helpful items); coordinating meals (assign others to do preparation and clean up); offering to stay at the house during the funeral; and helping with thank-you notes after Shiva.   — D.A.F.

Jewish tradition teaches that one does not attempt to console mourners prior to burial. During *aninut,* family and friends may offer assistance, but visitation prior to the funeral is generally avoided. The family of the deceased is busy with preparations and not prepared to receive condolences.

"Do not comfort mourners whose dead lies before them." (*Pirkei Avot* 4:18) While this may refer to the need to attend to practical matters before burial, it also speaks to the psychological dimensions of *aninut.* The period immediately following a death is typically one of emotional shock and numbness, and the reality and immensity of the loss has yet to sink in. The mourner is not yet able to think about a loved one in the past tense. Many grief experts suggest that concrete, task-oriented activities are the most appropriate during this period.   — B.R.

The funeral is often delayed until family members arrive. But in the interim period of *aninut,* mourners still need to receive comfort. Close friends and family may indeed be welcome visitors. Rather than following rigidly the restriction of *aninut,* we should be guided by what the mourners say would be helpful and appreciated even prior to the actual funeral.   — S.P.W.

Halvayat Hamet: *The Funeral*

Death is a time of isolation for mourners, softened by the presence of family and community. Judaism affirms that in death both the deceased and the mourners are not alone. The next stage in the journey of mourning is *halvayat hamet*, "accompanying the deceased" on his/her journey to the final resting place.

***Mitzvot* of *Avelut*/Mourning:** If a garment or ribbon has not previously been torn, the *k'ria*/tearing should take place at the funeral service.

In many communities, mourners sit in the front row of the place where the funeral is occurring, where they

People often ask whether they should bring children to a funeral. Death is more frightening in the abstract, and children cannot be protected from the reality of loss. A death affects the entire family, and the child is a member of the family. When children are mourners, and are old enough to be attentive and respectful, I usually encourage the family to include them in the tangible expressions of grief and farewell. However, friends may offer to stay with an infant or toddler who may distract the family members during a funeral. In some cases, family members may actually prefer the presence of a baby as a promise of hope and life.   — B.R.P.

Adults sometimes displace their own anxiety about funerals onto children, discouraging them from attending by anticipating that they will be upset. But death *is* upsetting. Children who are kept away from funerals will never have the memory of the event, of those who were present, of the words that were spoken and of the acts that were shared. They will not have the experience of knowing that we do not have to face a death alone. Deprived of this experience, children may not be given the opportunity, or feel there is permission, to grieve.   — R.H.

receive condolences prior to the funeral service. In other communities, the family enters the room only when the service is about to begin. Since these are only local customs, mourners should not feel compelled to comply with either model, but should choose what feels appropriate and comforting.

Mitzvot of **K'vod Hamet**/Honoring the Deceased: Funerals can take place anytime except on Shabbat and the first and last days of Jewish holidays. They normally take place during daylight hours. (For a discussion of funerals and Jewish holidays, see page 60.)

Jewish tradition mandates that the casket be closed for the funeral service as a sign of respect for the deceased, and as a way to encourage family and friends to remember the loved one as he or she was in life rather than in death. Public viewings and pre-funeral chapel visitations are not in keeping with Jewish tradition.

The custom in some communities of lining up to greet the bereaved family before the funeral service can impose a burden on mourners at their most vulnerable moment. Mourners should not feel obliged to engage in this custom. Those who wish to connect individually with the mourners might better—and more meaningfully—do so during Shiva.   — D.A.F.

One young widow of an active synagogue member, the mother of two young children, was very clear about her need to sit in the *middle* of the congregation at her husband's funeral. She felt less alone, deriving comfort from being surrounded (literally) by loved ones.   — S.P.W.

The body is treated with dignity, because it was literally the embodiment of a human life. While public viewings are not in keeping with Jewish tradition, some family members sometimes choose to view the body in a private setting prior to the funeral. This often happens if they arrived from a distance and want to have one last opportunity to see their loved one.   — D.E.

The funeral service liturgy is usually brief. Psalms, biblical passages and the memorial prayer *El Maley Rahamim* may be supplemented by selections from Jewish tradition, contemporary literature and poetry and other reflections. It is customary for a *hesped* (eulogy) to be offered in which the deceased is memorialized. Most often, this will be done by the rabbi, who either will have known the deceased or learned about her or him from the family. Sometimes, one or more members of the family may wish to speak briefly at the funeral service. In the interests of not overburdening family and friends with a lengthy service, the rabbi should always be consulted regarding additional speakers at a funeral.

The primary role of mourners at the funeral is to be mourners. Taking on the emotional task of speaking about a loved one during the highly charged time immediately before burial should be carefully considered. As an alternative, a relative or friend might be designated to offer remarks on behalf of the family, or to read remarks

Music soothes the soul and can provide an uplifting backdrop to a funeral. Cantorial music, folk tunes, a selection from a classical piece or a special song that says something important to the family might be considered. Though a family member may offer a vocal or instrumental rendition of a favorite song of the deceased, the stress of performing in such an emotional context may result in an awkward moment. Decisions about music appropriate to the setting should be discussed in advance with the rabbi or other officiant. In addition to the music offered by the rabbi or cantor, recorded music might be played as people enter or leave the chapel. This can be soothing and can leave a powerful impression.   — B.R.P./S.P.W.

Allow a minute or two of silence to invite mourners to hold a memory of the deceased in their heart and mind. This can be done as part of the eulogy or before reciting *El Maley Rahamim.*   — S.R.

prepared by one or more of the mourners. Mourners might consider, as an alternative, speaking briefly about the deceased during Shiva at home, prior to prayer services or prior to the recitation of the Kaddish.

Funerals most often take place in funeral parlor chapels, although some communities hold funerals in the synagogue. Graveside funerals, which combine the funeral and burial service, are also common.

When the casket is removed from the chapel, those present stand out of respect. Although local customs vary, in most communities the casket goes first in the procession from the chapel to the hearse and from the hearse to the grave upon reaching the cemetery.

In some communities, pallbearers have the actual responsibility for carrying the casket; elsewhere, the role is primarily honorary. Serving as a pallbearer is a custom rather than a law; anyone the family selects as appropriate may serve.

Mitzvot of *Niḥum Avelim*/Comforting the Mourners: Because funerals often take place close to midday and may involve considerable travel time, mourners may neglect to take care of their nutritional needs and can end up going a long time without food or drink. Add to this the stress of the death and funeral and any seasonal factors, such as extreme heat or cold, and mourners run the risk of weak-

---

In my experience, mourners (especially adult children) frequently want to speak at a funeral. While such participation should be carefully considered, it may well have a profound healing effect. It is often the case that a mourner who wrote a eulogy for a parent who was buried out of town will share it with the local community during Shiva. — S.P.W.

ening themselves or even becoming ill during the day of the funeral.

Those involved in supporting the mourners might prepare packages (sandwiches, snacks, drinks) for the mourners to take along during the ride to or from the funeral home or cemetery. Mourners often understandably overlook this and will appreciate the consideration.

At the funeral, friends and family provide comfort and consolation primarily by being present. There are few formal opportunities for people to convey condolences. When the funeral and burial are held separately, many people will often choose not to continue on to the cemetery after the service. Instead, they may try to seek out the mourners at the conclusion of the service. Although such interactions are meant to be comforting, they can be intrusive and stressful when mourners are in transition from the funeral to the cemetery. It is preferable to wait until a Shiva visit to offer condolences.

Halvayat Hamet: *The Burial*

The funeral is primarily a service of words; the burial is primarily a service of acts. Jewish tradition wisely recognizes the limits of language in confronting this life-boundary moment, and instead directs us to a series of acts with which to bring our loved ones to their final rest.

Mitzvot of *Avelut*/**Mourning:** The first time that mourners recite the Kaddish prayer is at the cemetery. Again, local customs vary: the Kaddish may be recited before or after the casket is lowered into the grave. (See page 51 for a full discussion of the Kaddish.)

Where contemporary culture often encourages us to divert our eyes when confronting death, Judaism encourages us to face the reality of mortality. A meaningful tradition is to help fill in the grave using the shovels that are

---

The recitation of the Mourner's Kaddish at the graveside marks the shift from a focus on the deceased to one that centers on the mourners. — D.E.

Be sure to ask the funeral director to arrange for an adequate amount of earth and for shovels, rather than a small symbolic trowel and a minimal mound of earth. — D.A.F.

Although the first sound of the earth landing on the casket may be startling, it often provides an emotional catharsis. The act of *k'vura* (burial) gives us a tangible way to mourn with our bodies in addition to our emotions. It is a deeply painful but profoundly moving act of love and respect. — L.P.

The sound of earth landing on the casket is unforgettable. It is the sound of finality, of grief and of the breaking heart. — Y.R.

usually provided. Family members are invited first, followed by any others who wish to do so. While this is often an intense emotional experience, it is also a confirmation and acceptance of the death. Burial is an act of *ḥesed shel emet* (selfless lovingkindness) on the part of the family and friends. It is an act that cannot be reciprocated by the deceased, and, as such, highlights the selflessness with which all *mitzvot* may be carried out.

It is the custom to replace the spade or shovel in the mound of earth rather than to hand it on to the next person. This may originate in a common belief found in almost all cultures, ancient as well as modern, that death is a contagion. Alternative explanations for retaining this custom might include: Each person had a different relationship with the deceased, and so each participates in the burial independently; or, by allowing each person to retrieve and then replace the spade or shovel, we offer each individual the opportunity to fulfill the *mitzva* of *k'vura*.

In some communities, it is customary to scatter earth from the Land of Israel into the grave, symbolically linking the life of the deceased to the life of the Jewish people, past, present and future. Funeral directors can usually provide small bags of earth from Israel.

Families are often anxious or encouraged to depart from the cemetery as soon as the service is concluded, but

---

The act of *k'vura* (burial) should be different from other moments when we might apply a shovel to the earth. In some communities, it is customary to invite the mourners first to use the back of the spade to move the earth onto the casket, and only then to place a few shovelfuls in the normal manner. This is a more difficult way to move the earth, and it underscores the sanctity—and the difficulty—of burying our loved ones.   — Y.R.

it is appropriate to remain at the grave at least until the casket is covered with earth, and preferably until the grave is filled in. However, the circumstances of the death, the emotional and physical condition of the mourners, and weather conditions should be taken into account.

The transition from the cemetery back to the home is poignant and profound. Before leaving the cemetery grounds, some follow the custom of plucking up a few strands of grass and tossing them over the shoulder. Many associate this practice with the biblical verse, "At daybreak, [we] are like grass that renews itself . . . [B]y dusk, it withers and dries up" (Psalms 90:5–6) or "God remembers that we are but dust" (Psalms 103:14).

Similarly, it is customary to wash one's hands upon leaving the cemetery or prior to reentering the home, depending on local and family customs. Some people do both. This practice is related to ancient traditions of washing as an act

The tradition of participating in the burial comes from a time when cemeteries did not employ staff for that purpose. Regardless of how much of the grave is filled in, or how long the mourners stay at the graveside, the underlying concern is the same: It is the obligation of family and friends to ensure that the burial of their loved ones takes place. After the burial ceremony is over, some choose to return to the graveside for individual reflection.   — D.E.

I have witnessed families performing k'vura (burial) with great love and dedication, insisting on completely filling in the grave before continuing. I have also observed families who moved away from the grave as the rabbi and others performed the minimal covering. People who can overcome the mixed emotions of this final farewell often find the act of filling the grave to be fulfilling and cathartic.   — B.R.P.

Burials can often reanimate feelings of grief or loss regarding other deceased family members. When the burial is completed, people can be encouraged to visit and place a stone on any other family graves in the cemetery as a source of comfort and as a way to connect the familial circles of life and death.   — Y.R.

of ritual purification. The acts of plucking grass and washing hands suggest a need to demarcate the boundary between death and life—the cemetery and the world outside the cemetery.

Mitzvot **of** *K'vod Hamet*/**Honoring the Deceased:** At the cemetery, the procession normally follows the casket. Tradition suggests that the procession pause several times (seven is the common number) before reaching the grave. Explanations for this custom include a reticence to take final leave of our loved ones, a desire to impress those present with the solemnity of the moment and an opportunity to reflect on our own mortality.

At the graveside, local customs vary: In some places, the casket is lowered into the grave before the final prayers are offered; in other locales, the casket remains at ground level until the liturgy is completed.

Jewish law mandates burial in the earth. The process of natural decomposition is considered the most gentle and appropriate. Burial in a mausoleum, while not customary in our day, is not prohibited by Jewish tradition and was apparently not uncommon in the early talmudic

---

At liminal moments, Jewish tradition often uses water to symbolize the passing of one stage of life and the beginning of another. On a primal level, we have the ability to flow between life and death. We rinse our hands with water as we leave the place where the dead are at rest and turn toward the places where life is present. The gentle flow of water over our hands—like the gentle wash of tears over our faces—can soften the rawness of bearing witness to death and burial. As we bid a final goodbye to the body of the departed, water can help soothe the harsh finality of death. The waters of the womb are where life begins; and, in the tradition of *tahara,* the waters of purification are where life ends. Water can thus signify cleansing and renewal, birth and rebirth, endings and beginnings.   — M.K.

period. In contemporary Jewish life, cremation is sometimes chosen in place of burial. (For a discussion of cremation, see page 57.)

Mitzvot of Niḥum Avelim/Comforting the Mourners: At the cemetery, when the service and the burial are complete and the mourners are preparing to leave, those present customarily form two parallel lines, creating a corridor of comfort for the mourners. It is often difficult to arrange people into this linear configuration without intruding on the emotional intensity of the moment. One way to assist is for the rabbi or other officiant to suggest that after individuals have an opportunity to place earth in the grave, they move into one of two lines leading from the graveside, to be ready to support the mourners on their journey from the cemetery. Those choosing not to place earth can be invited to step into a line as well.

Before or as the mourners pass through, it is customary for the rabbi and/or those offering comfort to say, *"Hamakom yinaḥem etkhem betokh sha'ar aveley tziyon virushalayim,"* "May God comfort you, along with all the mourners of Zion and Jerusalem." This ancient benediction links the life of each individual Jew to the life of the Jewish people and to the hope for a messianic future. The "mourners of Zion and Jerusalem" will be comforted when, according to traditional Jewish religious belief, the Messiah arrives and Jerusalem is rebuilt and the dead are resurrected. While Reconstructionist Judaism does not affirm belief

The first response to death in Jewish history was Abraham's acquiring a site for the burial of his wife, Sarah (Genesis 23).   — S.P.W.

in a personal Messiah or resurrection of the dead, the symbolism of a messianic age of peace and plenitude for all renders this traditional benediction appropriate.

Tradition not only recommends but actually requires that the mourners be served a meal as a sign of their recommitment to life, and of the necessity of beginning to resume normal routines at a time that is anything but normal. It is a *mitzva* of *niḥum avelim*/comforting the mourners for several people to stay behind at the Shiva home and prepare the traditional *se'udat havra'a*/meal of consolation so that upon returning from the cemetery, mourners can have some nourishment. Customary foods representing the circle and cycle of life include eggs and lentils. Meat and wine are avoided.

Those preparing the Shiva home for the return of the mourners should place a basin, a pitcher of water and towels outside the door for those who wish to do the customary handwashing when they return from the cemetery.

Forming two lines to flank mourners as they leave the graveside is a visible reminder of the caring and companionship that will accompany them through the journey of grieving and healing.   — D.A.F.

The use of the name *Hamaḳom* (literally, "The Place") for God in a prayer for comfort and healing speaks to me. *Hamaḳom*. The Place. Opening to this moment in all its mystery, dread, confusion, pain. Opening the heart to the possibility of its own ultimate power to receive comfort, if it does not hide or flee from *hamaḳom hazeh,* this place.   — S.P.W.

When I felt deep grief, I had no appetite. I almost felt like joining my beloved in the grave, rather than rejoining the world of ordinary life with its appetites. The meal of consolation forces mourners back to a primal connection with life, appetite, food and body, despite the often-experienced desire to remain faithful to the deceased in the realm of death.   — S.P.W.

Shiva: *The First Week*

Shiva ("seven") refers to the traditional period of time following burial that is set aside for mourners to receive condolences and be together. In the biblical tradition, seven is a number of wholeness and completion. The origin of seven days of mourning goes back to the earliest generations of the Jewish people, when Joseph mourned his father Jacob (Genesis 50:10).

Mitzvot **of** *Avelut/***Mourning:** Shiva begins when the burial is completed, and regardless of how close to sunset the burial may be, that counts as one day. Since Jewish days begin at sunset, the night of the day of the burial begins the second day of counting for Shiva, and so forth. If there is a cremation, it is recommended that Shiva begin from the conclusion of the funeral service prior to, or memorial service subsequent to, the cremation. On Shabbat, public observances of Shiva are suspended; the Kad-

In seven days heaven and earth and all they contain were created. In the seven days of Shiva, we acknowledge that creation is still present, still possible, despite the loss we have experienced. — S.P.W.

Though it may seem disconcerting to suspend public acts of mourning during Shabbat, those who find meaning in the separation of Shabbat from the rest of the week may experience this as a respite and a welcome reminder of the larger context of our lives. — B.R.P.

dish is recited in the synagogue. On Saturday night at sunset, Shiva observances resume. Shabbat is counted as one of the days of Shiva.

While Shiva literally means "seven," in many contemporary Jewish families circumstances and/or choice may result in a decision to reduce the number of days that Shiva is observed. In order to demonstrate respect for the deceased, and to allow mourners a reasonable period in which to be together and share their sadness, it is recommended that the minimum observance consist of not fewer than three days. Jewish law allows those who would be economically harmed by a longer absence to return to work after three days of Shiva.

In past generations, the family usually observed Shiva at the home of the deceased. However, any residence that works may be chosen. Mourners are free to sleep at home

---

The problems with choosing a full period of Shiva may include lost work and the possibility of feeling trapped within a mourning ritual for a longer period than feels comfortable. The problems with choosing a shortened period for Shiva may include disrupting a helpful mourning process and attempting to reengage with life prematurely. One of the benefits of tradition is to create a framework for behavior during times when we may not be able to think clearly for ourselves. The wisdom of allowing a full week to begin to absorb the loss in the daily rhythm of one's life is validated by centuries of tradition. If in doubt, simply accepting the traditional customs for counting the period for Shiva can eliminate one more decision during a difficult period.   — D.E.

There is an unfortunate tendency to abridge mourning practices when the person who died had lived for a very long time, or had struggled with a long illness. Loss does not need to be tragic in order to be profound. A 70-year-old daughter whose 95-year-old mother dies has had a mother through all of the phases of her life, and now may need to reorder her sense of the world and of herself. Mourners should give themselves ample opportunity to grieve and to be comforted.   — D.A.F.

and to come and go from the Shiva home as necessary, but outside trips (shopping, errands, social visits) should be avoided.

With the geographic dispersal of families, people often attend a funeral in a community far from their home. Some people observe part or all of Shiva in their home communities. Others choose to hold an additional one-day or one-night Shiva observance when they return home so that local friends and family who may not have been able to travel to the funeral can offer condolences.

At the beginning of Shiva, upon returning home from the cemetery, a candle that burns for seven days is lit in the Shiva home. There are differing explanations for this practice; a common one associates light with the soul—"the human soul is the light of God" (Proverbs 20:27). For many mourners, the candle is a symbol of the abiding presence of the memory of the deceased.

During Shiva, mourners refrain from domestic and professional work and generally restrict themselves to the

Shiva presumes that the mourner dwells in a different spiritual and emotional place than the rest of the world. Shiva prescribes a unique time and space so that the mourner may attend to the difficult but necessary work of mourning and inner healing. This approach is at odds with our careerist culture, where bereavement leave is often considered an indulgent luxury. What does it say about a society where too many find it unthinkable to ask for, or to take, the necessary time off to grieve the loss of a loved one?   — B.R.

I often have had to encourage people to have a local Shiva observance. Afterward, they are always grateful. It means so much to have neighbors and co-workers—your own people—gather around when the formal mourning has occurred away from home.   — S.P.W.

Shiva home and/or their own home. Mourners abstain from activities identified with recreation and pleasure. They avoid leather shoes and customarily sit on low stools or benches, or on chairs and/or sofas from which the cushions have been removed. Those for whom such seating is difficult, such as those with physical and/or medical conditions, including pregnancy, are exempt from this practice.

Cutting hair, shaving, using cosmetics and so forth are avoided during Shiva. Bathing for hygienic purposes is permissible. Sexual activity is avoided, because it stands in emotional contrast to death and mourning.

In many Shiva homes, the custom of covering mirrors is observed. The origins of this practice are likely to be found in ancient anxieties surrounding death and demons—the concern being that one's image or the soul of the deceased might be imprisoned in a mirror, or that a mirror might be an inadvertent gateway between the realms of life and death. Later Jewish tradition offers two other explanations. One suggests that looking at one's reflection induces vanity, considered inappropriate to the

---

The seven days of Shiva are like an island of time and space for the mourners, a kind of parallel universe. Being visited and comforted can be simultaneously helpful and overwhelming. Mourners should not have to serve as "hosts"; they should be able to receive visitors, as well as words of comfort. Keeping the door unlocked during the times that people visit, for example, allows people to come in and offer condolences without the mourner having to get up and welcome them. Since some visitors may not be familiar with this traditional practice, consider placing a note on the door telling people to come in without knocking.   — Y.R.

It will be appreciated if a few people volunteer to take care of the logistics of Shiva, including food preparation, cleaning up when the day's visits have concluded and other "hosting" activities.   — Y.R.

humility that mourning is expected to induce. The other suggests that a mourner who sees the reflection of a bedraggled appearance may be moved to shave or put on cosmetics in contradiction of Jewish tradition. While no single explanation can substantiate this or any other ritual practice, the emotional power of a tangible disruption of the normal appearance of the home (in ways similar to, for example, removing sofa and chair cushions so mourners can sit lower than usual) is an appropriate expression of the disruption in the family system created by the death.

Prayer services are usually held in the Shiva home. Since Jews are traditionally enjoined to pray three times daily and mourners do not attend the synagogue during Shiva (with the exception of Shabbat), it was imperative that they be enabled to pray by bringing the synagogue, as it were, into their home.

In many Reconstructionist communities, the custom is to hold services only in the evening, but services may also

At a time of Shiva, one sees oneself not in a mirror, but in the faces of those who come to offer consolation. Irrespective of its origins, the practice of covering mirrors can speak to the mourner. Part of one's self-image has, in some sense, died along with the deceased. A covered mirror is a tangible symbol of the loss of part of oneself. It provides a reminder that the world that previously mirrored the self is now different. It confirms that Shiva is a time of emptiness and loss, in which the world often seems veiled. Another "self" is being shaped, one that we will see for the first time when we uncover the mirrors at the end of Shiva. — M.K.

For most liberal Jews, the daily prayer service is not a regular aspect of the daily routine. Nevertheless, having a Shiva minyan at home can be a source of comforting reflection and communal support. Community members, even if they are not close to the grieving family, can offer comfort by bringing prayerbooks, joining in the chanting of the prayers and hearing stories about the deceased. — B.R.P.

be held in the morning. If a family chooses not to hold a formal religious service at the home during Shiva, it is recommended that some structured period of brief Torah study—the reading of part of the weekly Torah portion or other biblical passages, perhaps some of the Psalms—be offered instead. Both prayer and study are appropriate as a prelude to the mourners' recitation of the Kaddish.

On the last day of Shiva, formal mourning practices conclude ("getting up from Shiva"), either following the morning service (if one is held) or sometime between early morning and midday. A traditional practice is for mourners take a walk outside as a symbol of stepping back into the routines that were suspended during Shiva. (See "Conclusion of Shiva," p. 74.)

Some mourners elect to have services exclusively in the morning. A morning service can help the mourners to face the day. Morning services may also allow children with early bedtimes to participate. — L.P.

Some choose to ask mourners and/or visitors to share thoughts and memories of the deceased before, during or after a Shiva service. For gatherings where those present are unfamiliar with Jewish liturgy, this might even be done in lieu of formal worship. — B.R.

Getting up from Shiva can be a wrenching experience. As we leave the shelter that shielded us from work, business and social obligations, it is easy to feel overwhelmed. The absence of our loved one becomes more palpable when the intensely communal experience of Shiva is over. It is important to be gentle with ourselves on reentry, to expect that we will not immediately work or function at our normal capacity and to accept that we will continue to need and deserve support for some time. — D.A.F.

Biblical tradition speaks of how at the moment of death one is "gathered to his (her) ancestors." Prior to going for a walk marking the end of Shiva, I ask those present to name their "ancestors" with whom the deceased is now gathered. — S.R.

If you take a walk to mark the end of Shiva, consider who you would like to accompany you. On the walk, you might discuss the experience of Shiva, any lessons learned and what you imagine lies ahead. — D.E.

Traditional Jewish laws regarding Shiva and Jewish holidays are complex. For a discussion of Shiva and Jewish holidays, see page 60.

Mitzvot of *K'vod Hamet*/Honoring the Deceased: During Shiva, it is customary to honor the memory of the deceased by telling stories of her/his life and sharing memorabilia, including photographs and video/audio. Many of those coming to offer comfort during Shiva may not have known the deceased. This is an opportunity to honor her/his memory by recounting something of her/his life.

Mitzvot of *Niḥum Avelim*/Comforting the Mourners: It is appropriate to visit the Shiva home to offer condolences and express sympathy for the loss. Sharing memories of the deceased person is also appropriate. Mourners often remember the presence of comforters rather than the words they say. Just sitting with people and providing a sense of solidarity is often enough.

The atmosphere at a Shiva home should reflect the emotional reality of the family's loss. While serious, it need not always be somber, although solemnity is appropriate when confronting a tragic loss. While all deaths are sad, there are those that come with peace and calm at the end of a long life, and at Shiva the family may warmly

---

Traditionally, when paying a Shiva call, a visitor does not speak unless or until a mourner has spoken first. In contemporary life, adherence to this practice is often awkward for the visitor, the mourner, or both. An alternative is for a visitor to offer an initial expression of condolence (for example, "I am sorry for your loss"), and then let the mourner set the tone. The mourner may not want, or need, to engage in further conversation. Visitors often feel at a loss for words, but it may not be necessary to say anything more, since simply being present can speak volumes to a mourner. — Y.R.

share memories in celebration of the life. Other losses, including sudden and early deaths, accidental deaths and other shocking tragedies should be reflected in the tone of the Shiva home. Friends coming to visit should support the family and recognize their needs and avoid engaging in conversations of a social or business nature that can easily be deferred until outside the Shiva home.

Helping prepare meals, doing light housekeeping, and volunteering for errands such as shopping and transporting children are all helpful ways of supporting mourners.

Sheloshim: *The First Month*

The thirty days after the funeral/burial are called *sheloshim* ("thirty"). For the mourning of all immediate relatives except parents, this period comprises and concludes formal mourning observances. For parents, mourners continue a series of observances for a period of eleven months. (See page 38.)

Many contemporary Jews experience losses of other relatives, such as a spouse, a sibling or a child as equal to (or even greater than) the loss of a parent, and thus choose to continue observing certain mourning practices, espe-

---

The early days after a death are times of strong, even overpowering, emotions. Anger and guilt are almost inevitable concomitants of loss. These feelings are free-floating; they tend to find a thing or person to which to attach. For example, mourners may be angry at a doctor, at a funeral director, at a family member or at a rabbi. At base, however, the anger might be about being robbed of a loved one, perhaps while there was unfinished business in the relationship. Mourners may feel guilty for what they did or did not do or say to the deceased, even when observers would suggest that they acted with exemplary devotion. Such guilt is existential—we have survived, while our loved one has not. Practicing compassion and forgiveness—for ourselves, for the deceased and for those around us—may be helpful and healing.   — D.A.F.

Sheloshim is a demarcation without great ritual reinforcement. Shiva comes to an end, but we are still easing ourselves back into the routines of life. We struggle to reengage with life before we have fully assimilated the death that has occurred. The "time out of time" feeling of Shiva gives way to normal routines, tasks and appointments. Marking the end of *sheloshim* with a service or memorial gathering can help illuminate the journey traveled during the first month after a loss.   — D.E.

cially the recitation of the Kaddish, beyond *sheloshim* and even up to the full eleven months normally reserved for the loss of a parent.

Mitzvot of *Avelut*/Mourning: The first month following death is a period of adjustment during which the intensity of the loss starts to recede as mourners begin to return to the rhythms of their lives. Following the conclusion of Shiva, mourners can return to their regular professional and domestic work patterns. Mourners no longer sit on low stools, cover mirrors, wear a torn garment/black ribbon, avoid sexual relations or refrain from shaving.

However, it is customary for mourners to retain some outward observances. During *sheloshim*, mourners usually avoid parties, celebrations and public entertainment. One can attend Bar/Bat Mitzva services, weddings and other life-cycle events, but may choose not to attend the celebrations often attached to those rituals. It is customary to avoid wearing new clothing during *sheloshim*. Mourners continue to recite Kaddish during this period. It is customary to conclude *sheloshim* with a gathering of friends and family in which words of Torah are exchanged and studied in honor of the deceased.

Mitzvot of *K'vod Hamet*/Honoring the Deceased: The settling of the estate of the deceased, closing of her/his residence and disposition of her/his property often occur during *sheloshim*. While emotionally difficult for mourners, these necessary activities are part of the process of accepting and working through the loss. (See "A Ritual for Closing a Home After a Death," p. 81.)

When we invoke the name of a person who is deceased, it is customary to add *"alav hashalom"* (for a male) or *"aleha hashalom"* (for a female) ("peace be upon him/ her") after the name. Another phrase often used is *"zikhrono livrakha"* (for a male) or *"zikhrona livrakha"* (for a female) ("his/her memory is a blessing").

Mitzvot of Niḥum Avelim/Comforting the Mourners: After the funeral and Shiva, as visitations end, mourners are often unintentionally abandoned. While free to resume their normal home and work lives, mourners, in differing degrees, may still want or need support and assistance. Phone calls, letters and brief visits may all be appropriate and appreciated. Invitations for Shabbat and/or holiday meals may help. Offering to attend synagogue services with mourners, especially those who are alone, can help prevent the isolation that often settles on surviving spouses. In general, friends should check in with mourners during *sheloshim* to see how they are and if they need anything.

Although the immediacy of death recedes, grieving continues. Mourners continue the process of moving through their time of loss. Marking the end of the *sheloshim* period with a gathering provides a prayerful context in which the blessings of the life of the deceased that are now emerging as sacred memories can be recounted. Studying and/or teaching Torah in the deceased's honor and honoring the Torah of his/her life by sharing stories of that life can be potent rituals for mourners working on integrating their loss into the life they are currently reconstructing. — M.K.

Mourners who observed Shiva away from home will not have had the opportunity to acknowledge ritually their loss with their own community. A memorial service at the conclusion of *sheloshim* is an opportunity to gather with that community. Sometimes, mourners have observed Shiva in another city or state, and have not had the opportunity to acknowledge their loss ritually with their home community. A memorial service at the conclusion of *sheloshim* is an opportunity for individuals to gather with that community. — B.R.

Yahrtzeit: *The First Year*

The journey of mourning does not always follow a level pathway. As time goes by, the intensity of grieving may diminish. But at significant moments in the year, such as birthdays, holidays and anniversaries, mourners may find themselves revisiting their loss as if it happened only yesterday.

Mitzvot of *Avelut*/Mourning: When one is mourning for a parent, it is customary to extend certain practices beyond the thirty days of *sheloshim* to a full twelve months. Most common is the recitation of the Kaddish (although the Kaddish is recited daily only for eleven months) followed by avoidance of public celebrations and entertainment. When mourners choose to extend mourning beyond *sheloshim* for other relatives, these practices may similarly be extended. The counting of the twelve months of mourning, including the eleven months of recitation of the Kaddish, begins from the date of the death, not the date of the funeral. In a Jewish leap year, there will be thirteen months, but mourning practices are carried out only for twelve.

The twelve months of mourning serve an important purpose. Mourners need to experience the full year's cycle without the presence of their loved one—including birthdays, anniversaries, holidays and other moments of significance—in order to absorb the loss fully into their lives.

The tradition of reciting the Kaddish for only the first eleven of the twelve months derives from certain rabbinic teachings that associate the year following death as a period of purgation for the soul of the deceased in anticipation of the soul's return to God. These teachings associate the recitation of the Kaddish during that time as aiding the cleansing of the soul. To avoid implying that the soul of the deceased was so severely tainted as to require a full year of mourning, a tradition evolved to conclude formal mourning practices after eleven months. A historical perspective would suggest that the eleven-month period preceded any attempts to explain its origins. Once the practice became standard, attempts were made to explain a custom that had already attained communal consensus.

An alternative explanation may be found in the analogy of Shiva ending on the morning of the seventh day rather than at sunset. As the first year following the death comes near to its conclusion, we abridge the fullness of twelve months and conclude, instead, just as the last month of the first year is beginning. In so doing, we glimpse the Jewish affirmation of life over death.

Adults mourning an abusive parent have sometimes chosen to say the Kaddish for a full 12 months in an effort to embrace both the *mitzva* of *avelut,* and the reality of their experience with that parent.   — L.P.

Talmudic tradition teaches that the soul undergoes a process of postmortem purgation in Gehenna that lasts a maximum of twelve months (Babylonian Talmud, Rosh Hashana 17a; Shabbat 33b). Rabbi Moses b. Israel Isserles (1525–1572) limited the recitation of the Kaddish to eleven months, claiming that one would not want to assume his or her parent had deserved the maximum punishment in Gehenna.   — S.R.

Before the first anniversary of the loss, we give ourselves a full month to begin the transition back to normal activities as the restrictions of mourning recede. When we do, in fact, reach the first anniversary of the loss, we come to it with life renewed rather than in mourning.

The first anniversary of the loss is the first observance of the *yahrtzeit*. A Yiddish word meaning "year's time," *yahrtzeit* is observed on the anniversary of the date of death (not the date of burial), reckoned according to the Jewish calendar. Since Jewish days start at sunset, calculating the *yahrtzeit* date requires knowing if the death occurred before or after nightfall. If after, the date for the *yahrtzeit* will be the next day on the Jewish calendar. Rabbis can assist in determining the Jewish date of the *yahrtzeit* if the family knows the English date and time of death.

The first *yahrtzeit* has a unique significance. Mourners inevitably evoke memories of the day of their loss; the presence of their loved one may feel more tangible; memories may be intensely present, and there can be a recurrence of feelings of grief and sadness that had dissipated during the year.

The Internet has several sites that offer calculators (or guides) for converting yahrtzeit dates from the civil calendar to the Jewish calendar. Search the Internet for "*yahrtzeit* calculator." — D.Z.

Some mourners feel a need to create ritual around the civil calendar anniversary of the date of death, either in addition to or in place of the anniversary on the Jewish calendar. Traditional and/or innovative practices for *yahrtzeit* may be observed; family members, including children, can be invited to suggest ways to remember the deceased. — L.P.

The practices associated with *yahrtzeit* are customarily observed by those who were the mourners. Other family members, such as grandchildren, may also choose to observe a *yahrtzeit*. If those who are obligated to mourn have died, others in the family may step in and commit themselves to continuing the observance.

A memorial candle is kindled in the home the evening preceding the date of the *yahrtzeit*. While Jewish tradition does not provide a specific liturgy for this ritual, contemporary Jews have created a number of meditations, prayers and blessings. Personal reflections, a poem, a reading or a song are all appropriate as well. (See page 79.)

Yahrtzeits are also marked by the recitation of the Kaddish. Traditionally, this is done on the actual *yahrtzeit* day if mourners can attend a daily worship service for any or all of the three customary daily prayer services. In many communities, *yahrtzeits* are announced at Shabbat services, and

Young children may be well aware of the imminent arrival of a first *yahrtzeit,* especially of a parent. They may associate the date with the one on the civil calendar, which, depending on the year, can come before or after (or on) the *yahrtzeit* on the Hebrew calendar. It can be helpful to have some formal observance on both dates, as emotions can easily surface in both contexts. Possible observances might include lighting a *yahrtzeit* candle, looking through a photo album, making a *tzedaka* donation, and/or attending synagogue and reciting the Kaddish. It is helpful for a parent and/or other relatives to discuss in advance with a child what will be observed on the first *yahrtzeit,* and to invite the child to make suggestions as well. This signals to the child that the adult is aware that the date is approaching, and that it is to be expected that strong and sad feelings may be stirred up. Just as ritual helps by giving us something structured to do when a death occurs, ritual can transform a first *yahrzeit* into a paradigm, one that includes healing memories along with the acknowledgment of the reality of loss. — R.H.

those observing *yahrtzeit* any time within seven days recite the Kaddish. Local customs vary regarding whether recitation of the Kaddish should occur on the Shabbat before or after the *yahrtzeit* date. Check with the rabbi/congregation as to the practices in a given community. Many communities follow the custom of offering those observing *yahrtzeit* an *aliya* (recitation of blessings over the reading of the Torah) and/or designating one of the *aliyot*/Torah reading sections for anyone observing a *yahrtzeit* that week.

It is customary to make contributions of *tzedaka* and/or to engage in learning/teaching of Torah on a *yahrtzeit* in honor of the memory of the deceased. The *yahrtzeit* continues to be observed each year on the anniversary date.

***Mitzvot* of *K'vod Hamet*/Honoring the Deceased:** Families normally arrange for a headstone, monument or marker to be inscribed, erected and dedicated at the burial site. Monuments usually carry the English and Hebrew names of the deceased, as well as the English and Hebrew dates of birth and death. Families may choose a brief additional inscription. Check with a rabbi regarding the accurate spelling of Hebrew names, dates and/or phrases.

Since headstone dedications are in the realm of custom and not law, considerable latitude can be taken in deciding when to erect a monument. Mourners do need time to adjust to their loss. A dedication which occurs in close proximity to the funeral (anytime from *sheloshim* to approximately six months following the loss) will often evoke much of the emotion of the funeral itself, and mourners may feel as if they are experiencing a second round of grieving. It is recommended that dedications take place sometime in the second half of the year following a death. Seasonal and climatic factors can and should be taken into account.

Family events, whether informal or formal, often provide an opportunity for a dedication. For example, in today's Jewish community, the Friday preceding or Sunday following a Bar or Bat Mitzva is often used for dedications. Individuals and families should assess the emotional impact on families (and especially on Bar and Bat Mitzva students) of holding a dedication in proximity to a family celebration.

There is little formal liturgy associated with dedications. It is customary to recite the memorial prayer *El Maley Raḥamim* ("God full of compassion") in Hebrew and/or English, as well as the Kaddish. Psalms, readings, poems and/or family reflections can be shared as well. (See page 75 for a sample ritual.)

One custom is to set the date of the unveiling to coincide with the end of the eleven-month period of reciting the Kaddish. The unveiling then becomes a marker in time as well as a ceremony to dedicate the headstone.   — D.E.

It is not necessary to have a rabbi or cantor for an unveiling. One approach is to invite those present to share a memory or an aspect of the deceased. The weaving of memories reflects a tangible and ongoing connection to the deeds and spirit of our loved ones.   — D.A.F.

The tone of an unveiling service is demonstrably different from that of a funeral. The reality of loss has now become part of the fabric of the mourners' lives. We might view the unveiling as akin to the removal of a bandage—an acknowledgment of the healing process that has been at work since the loss occurred.   — B.R.

Mitzvot of *Niḥum Avelim*/Comforting the Mourners: Friends should stay in touch with mourners during the year after a loss. While there may be a decreasing need for specific support, the constancy of friendship is important. Widows and widowers often report that in the year following the loss of their partner/spouse, they experienced the loss of friendships with couples who may not have known how to adjust. Friends may also intervene if they observe that the mourner might need some additional support in adjusting to the loss, and may want to suggest some form of counseling.

Hazkarat Neshamot:
The Memorializing of Souls

After the conclusion of a first *yahrtzeit,* deceased relatives are remembered during the Yizkor service on the holidays of Pesaḥ, Sukkot-Shemini Atzeret, Shavuot and Yom Kippur. Recited in the synagogue, the Yizkor service allows personal losses to be shared with the community; we join with all who have taken the journey of mourning, those who have experienced recent losses and those who memorialize relatives who are long gone. Invisible presences join us as memories are evoked, names remembered and prayers offered.

On the holidays when Yizkor is recited, it is customary to light a memorial *(yahrtzeit)* candle in the home in the evening as the holiday begins, prior to kindling the festival candles.

Donations to a synagogue or other forms of *tzedaka* honor the memory of a loved one at times of *yahrtzeit* and Yizkor. Choosing a particular beneficiary can serve to continue a life mission or to create a legacy. When lighting the memorial light for my father, we share memories and reflect on events in the world and qualities in our children that he would have enjoyed. — B.R.P.

Bitzror Haḥayim: *The Bond of Life*

Jewish tradition is remarkably diverse in its perspectives on what happens after death. As an evolving religious tradition, Judaism has passed through several stages in its thinking about the afterlife. In the biblical period, the religion of ancient Israel reflected a variety of perspectives. While the meaning of life was understood primarily in this-worldly terms, the Bible shows evidence of some forms of belief in life beyond death.

The afterlife was sometimes envisioned as a shadowy and ethereal post-mortem existence (see, for example, I Samuel 28:11–19). The term *she'ol* is used a number of times to refer to the abode of the dead (see, for example, Numbers 16:30, Psalms 88:4; Job 7:9) One evocative passage in the book of the prophet Ezekiel (chapter 37) seems to suggest that some held an early belief in resurrection, although such passages were often understood to refer to the eternality of the collective Israelite community.

With the beginning of the transition to what would become the rabbinic period (two centuries before the Common Era), a more focused concern on the fate of the individual emerged. Evidence from this period in the later books of the Bible such as the book of Daniel, in the apocryphal books of the Maccabees and in early descriptions of Jewish liturgy, points to an emerging belief in *teḥiyat hametim*/resurrection of the dead and in *olam haba*/the [heavenly] world to come. The influence of Greek culture is seen in the perspectives of those who affirmed the eternality of the soul while denying the resurrection of the body. The rabbinic tradition reflected in the Talmud and the core of what became traditional Jewish liturgy saw the belief in resurrection—in which there was no ultimate body-soul dualism—as normative.

In medieval Jewish mysticism (Kabbalah), one can see increased attention to and concern about the nature and state of the soul. From the 12th century on, the belief in *gilgul neshamot* (reincarnation) became popular, and even prevalent, in certain Ashkenazic and Sefardic communities. This belief surfaced in early Hasidic thought as well.

From the rabbinic period until the advent of modernity, whatever individual Jews may have believed about life after death—bodily resurrection, a heavenly world to come, eternal souls, reincarnation, or any number of variants on these themes—classical Jewish liturgy affirmed that God was *meḥayey hametim,* the "One who revives the dead."

With the coming of modernity, the belief in bodily resurrection and a heavenly realm receded in the face of the rise of science, reason and rationality. The Reform and Reconstructionist prayerbooks eliminated references to resurrection and the world to come. The language of the current Reconstructionist liturgy affirms that God is *meḥayey kol ḥay* the "Fount of Life, who gives and renews life."

While no longer affirming many of the traditional ideas about life beyond death, Reconstructionist Judaism recognizes that eternality and immortality remain important spiritual concepts that can be understood from naturalistic and humanistic perspectives. Like our biblical ancestors, we can affirm faith in the eternality of the Jewish people. Our journey through life as Jews contributes to the totality of what the Jewish people has been and will become. Through our commitments and contributions, we can leave a legacy that strengthens and supports the Torah tradition as it is handed on to succeeding generations. And, like many of our ancestors, we affirm that beyond the limits of human life are our individual *neshamot*/souls with which we are graced and for which we are responsible. At death, the body comes to rest, but the soul is gathered back into the Godly dimension of existence.

Some Reconstructionists believe that the soul literally survives, cared for by a God capable of calling life itself into being, and capable of preserving it beyond its earthly journey. For other Reconstructionists, immortality is conferred through memory, as the values we lived by and the contributions we made to family, friends and the world are honored by those who live on after us. Some understand each soul to be as a wave, drawn back into the ocean from which it was essentially never separate. A smaller number of Reconstructionists no doubt find comfort and meaning in the more traditional ideas of a world to come where the injustices of this world are made right and the peace for which we long is finally bestowed.

Jewish life today is as diverse as it has been in any of the preceding three millennia. While religious movements in

Judaism may affirm or alter traditional ideas, individual Jews will choose what they believe about life beyond death—regardless of their denominational affiliation. In such a highly personal area of spiritual conviction, that is entirely appropriate. There is a wonderful diversity of Jewish views on life beyond death, and a remarkable humility in Judaism, which affirms that in ways we can never quite know—and perhaps do not need to know—the sacredness of human life transcends and survives beyond death.

Issues Related To Mourning

A. Who is a Mourner?

Jewish tradition defines a mourner as anyone having a first-degree relationship to the deceased: parents, spouses, children and siblings. While sadness and grieving extend throughout a family system, only those in primary relationships to the deceased are *obligated* to observe the Jewish ritual practices of mourning.

So, while grandchildren grieve the loss of grandparents, grandchildren are not obligated, for example, to observe Shiva or recite the Kaddish—although as participants in the family system at a time of loss, they obviously partake of the atmosphere of sadness. Similarly, in-laws may experience a sense of loss, but are not obligated as mourners.

Family members who are not obligated as mourners often voluntarily assume some of the obligations of

---

Who has "an obligation to mourn?" One might be a "mourner" even in the absence of a halakhic obligation. Although Jewish tradition did not anticipate "families by choice" as they exist in contemporary society, it did perceive the obligations that those bound by acknowledged commitments bear to one another in death as in life. Today, families and relationships appear in covenanted constellations that go beyond what tradition anticipated. There are profound ways in which one who had been engaged in a relationship of depth and responsibility may find reciting the Kaddish to be a meaningful and authentic choice to uphold.   — M.K.

mourning. In cases where, for example, no one is left to mourn or say the Kaddish for a certain relative—or, if no one else in the family shares the Jewish commitments that would support such observance—another relative might take on the *mitzvot* of mourning, including recitation of the Kaddish, for that deceased relative. Another example might be a grandchild who was exceptionally close to a deceased grandparent, and who, out of affection and respect, chooses to offer the Kaddish for her/him during the period after death. There is nothing wrong with voluntarily taking on certain observances that are not required.

B. The Kaddish

The Kaddish prayer originated in the days of the Talmud (c. 100–500 CE). The earliest form, the *Kaddish Derabanan* ("the Kaddish over study"), was originally offered to conclude a period of Torah learning; it had no connection with death and mourning. Over the generations, several versions of the Kaddish developed. Some versions, such as the *Ḥatzi Kaddish* (abridged Kaddish) and the *Kaddish Shalem* (expanded Kaddish) appear in synagogue liturgy at punctuation points between sections of the services.

Partners in same-sex relationships can have loving spousal relationships equal in meaning to those shared by heterosexual life-partners. When a loss occurs, a partner may not only feel drawn to the obligations of mourning, but in keeping with Reconstructionist Judaism's affirmations of equality for gay men and lesbians, would be encouraged to act on those feelings and observe the rituals of mourning.   — M.K.

The *Kaddish Yatom,* or Mourner's Kaddish that we associate with mourning observances, gradually emerged in the Middle Ages. In addition to recitation at the burial and during the subsequent mourning period, the Kaddish is also recited on a *yahrtzeit* (anniversary of a death) and at *Yizkor* (synagogue memorial service held on Pesaḥ Shavuot, Sukkot-Shemini Atzeret and Yom Kippur).

There is one version known as the burial Kaddish, which, in fact, makes reference to death, but it is rarely recited because it includes unfamiliar phrases that can disrupt an average mourner's recitation. The Kaddish with which most Jews are familiar does not mention death at all, but is rather an affirmation of the Godliness that inheres in life itself despite the boundaries of life. It is an affirmation that while a life has come to an end, life itself continues on with all its possibilities for the future. Perhaps that is why the prevailing theme of the Kaddish is the hope for the coming of a world governed by Godliness.

1. Who recites the Kaddish?

Jewish tradition differentiates between those *obligated* as mourners and those who may voluntarily *choose* to adopt some or all of the requirements of mourning. The Kaddish is traditionally understood as an obligation only of first-degree family members—the same people who are obligated to observe Shiva. While some Jews have retained the folk practice of engaging someone to recite the Kaddish on behalf of their deceased, Reconstructionist Judaism expects mourners themselves to take responsibility for this *mitzva.*

In many communities, it has become the custom in synagogue services for everyone to recite the Kaddish. While some Jews may find this solidarity to be a source of comfort, there is wisdom in allowing the mourners to recite the Kaddish alone, especially at the burial and during Shiva. It is their first formal act of mourning, inaugurating the Shiva; it is a time when they do truly stand apart from everyone else because of their relationship to the deceased; it is an affirmation among them of what binds them as a family. The Kaddish is not a prayer intended for all people in general, but for individual people in particular.

Although often based on a well-intentioned desire to provide support to those in mourning or observing a *yahrtzeit,* the communal recitation of the *Kaddish Yatom* deprives the ritual of much of its significance as a life-cycle event for an individual. Would anyone seriously suggest, in the interest of providing support to a nervous 13-year-old, that the congregation should join in the chanting of the Bar or Bat Mitzva's first Torah blessing? A mourner's recitation of the Kaddish should not be obscured or diminished by being absorbed into a congregational recitation. The act of support that is generally cited as justification for communal recitation is already present in the traditional call and response of the *Kaddish Yatom,* where the mourners lead and the community responds with *"y'hey sh'mey raba . . ."* and with *"amen."* We should recognize the wisdom of our ancestors and restore recitation of the Kaddish to individuals who are in mourning or who are observing a *yahrtzeit.* — D.G.C.

Some communities have a practice that they believe provides support while also preserving the meaningful distinction between mourners and non-mourners. The mourners begin the Kaddish recitation, but the community then rises and joins in on the response line *("y'hey sh'mey raba . . .")* and continues in solidarity with the mourners to the end. — L.P.

We do not truly support mourners by standing with them at the time of Kaddish. Mourners need their grief to be seen and acknowledged by others, and standing to say the Kaddish provides this visibility and acknowledgement. But when all members of the congregation stand to recite Kaddish, mourners instantly become invisible and unseen. Congregations should be encouraged to eliminate this practice, and find other ways to lend support and solidarity to those in mourning. — S.R.

2. How long does one recite the Kaddish?

Jewish tradition wisely demarcates an outside boundary for formal mourning, suggesting that while grieving is both necessary and appropriate, reentering life after loss is also important. Tradition says that for a parent, one recites the Kaddish for eleven months, counting from the day of the burial. For all other relatives for whom one is obligated to mourn, the Kaddish is to be recited for thirty days, again counting from the burial. Many Jews find it appropriate to recite the Kaddish beyond thirty days for non-parent relatives. While there is no obligation to do so, one certainly may if it provides comfort and helps on the journey through mourning. The outside boundary for regular recitation of Kaddish as a mourner is eleven months. Long-term memorialization of loved ones should be found in acts undertaken in their name and memory.

What if a parent makes clear the desire to have a child say the Kaddish, but the child finds the observance of the ritual not to be emotionally satisfying, or even oppressive? On the other hand, what if a parent makes clear that he or she considers recitation of the the Kaddish superstitious nonsense and directs a child *not* to observe the ritual, but the child wants to recite the Kaddish in order to satisfy his or her emotional and spiritual needs? Tradition suggests that children are not obligated to observe the wishes of parents when doing so would contravene *halakha* (a perspective that sometimes influences children struggling over whether to honor a parent's request for cremation, for example). But for those who look to the tradition for guidance but not for governance, such teachings are one piece among others to be considered and weighed.

— D.G.C.

3. *Kaddish without a Minyan:*

The Kaddish is among the prayers that traditionally require a *minyan* (prayer quorum of ten adult Jews) for recitation. One reason that comforters assemble at a Shiva home is to allow mourners to recite the Kaddish as part of prayer services.

In light of contemporary needs and people's work and family schedules, it is often difficult for mourners to attend a scheduled service at a synagogue in order to recite the Kaddish following Shiva. The question arises as to whether an individual might recite the Kaddish in the absence of a *minyan,* on a private basis, if s/he cannot attend synagogue to do so.

Mourners during their period of formal mourning share a solidarity that is most tangible when they join with other mourners in reciting the Kaddish in congregational services. Many mourners testify to the comfort provided by regular (if not always daily) attendance at services, even if prior to the death in their family they did not regularly attend synagogue. In many ways, the extra effort necessary to fit synagogue attendance into one's schedule is rewarded by a sense of calm, by new friendships made and by an awareness that even in a period of need, one also contributes to a community that relies on people showing up for each other.

However, in light of personal, professional, partnering and parenting schedules, it is difficult for many people to maintain even the best-intentioned commitments toward daily synagogue attendance. Additionally, it is a reality of the contemporary Jewish community that many congregations do not schedule daily services, forcing people who want to recite the Kaddish daily to attend services in a congregation other than their own.

Individual recitation of the Kaddish, even in the absence of a *minyan,* does help maintain a pattern of ritual and regularity that is part of the journey of mourning. While joining with a community for prayer is optimal, if mourners cannot manage daily synagogue attendance and/or if their congregation does not provide for daily prayer services, then the Kaddish can be recited on a private basis. Since most congregations do hold services on Shabbat, mourners should make every effort to join their communities on Shabbat evening and/or Shabbat morning to recite the Kaddish within the community.

Since the Kaddish originated as a prayer marking the conclusion of a period of Torah study, it is also appropriate, either in addition to or perhaps in place of the recita-

Some individuals seek a Kaddish practice that connects them to their deceased loved one's particular life and teaching. For example, one woman felt that the best way to honor her mother, an accomplished knitter, would be to dedicate a period of time each day to knitting. She used that special time to connect with her mother's love and legacy. One man chose to say the Kaddish after a daily period of writing dedicated to his deceased father's life and legacy.   — D.A.F.

A meditative practice of Kaddish: Allow yourself to sit quietly and breathe gently in and out. Bring to your mind's eye the image of the departed. See the eyes, the face, the body. Notice shifts in your own body as you deepen in this meditation. As you breathe in, take in the blessings that the memories of this person bring to you today. As you breathe out, send out the blessings of those memories in your wishes for a world uplifted by the departed having been a part of it. Continue this practice for several breaths. When you have completed this process, you might choose to conclude your meditation with the Kaddish, and/or with a poem or other writing that expresses something of the essence of the departed that you want to remember.
   — M.K.

tion of the Kaddish (depending on individual comfort levels) for mourners to set aside a few minutes each day for some form of Torah study. In addition to the weekly Torah portion or biblical texts such as the Psalms, mourners might consult any number of publications that offer Jewish "thoughts for a day," some of which are specifically written for the observance of a period of mourning.

C. Cremation

Cremation is a complex issue. Jewish law is unequivocal in prohibiting cremation: Burial in the earth is the norm. The earliest chapters of the Torah are invoked in support of this practice. The name *Adam* ("Earthling/Human") derives from the noun *adama* (earth, humus), and the

In addition to saying the Kaddish, there is also a subtle, internal "Kaddish process" that takes place during the year of mourning. Grief entails a process of sifting through one's feelings for and memories of the deceased, moving from the pain of mourning toward a sense of meaning, from emotional longing toward an acknowledgement of the legacy of spirit of the one who has died. If one cannot find the time, or a community, for saying the Kaddish, mourners can be encouraged to find private time to honor "the Kaddish process"—to find ways to mourn and memorialize the deceased. That private time might consist of activities such as journal writing, quiet contemplation, viewing photographs of the deceased, listening to special music, taking a meditative walk or saying the Kaddish alone. — S.R.

There is yet another traditional rationale for Judaism's antipathy toward cremation: the value of *k'vod hamet,* an attitude of respect and honor given to the human body, which is viewed as sacred and God-given. Our bodies do not ultimately belong to us: they are divine gifts, the sacred houses of our souls. As we are obligated to care for and respect our bodies while alive, others are expected to do so for us after we die. We, in effect, borrow our bodies for but a temporary period, and we are bidden to return them with respect and appreciation. — B.R.

Torah teaches that "dust you are and to dust you shall return" (Genesis 3:10). The Jewish belief in bodily resurrection, which was common until the advent of modernity, also likely influenced the prohibition against cremation.

While Reconstructionist Judaism does not affirm resurrection of the body, other contemporary concerns inform discussions regarding cremation. Prominent among them is the evocative agony of the Holocaust. Jews living in the post-Holocaust era cannot escape the association of cremation with the annihilation of European Jewry during the Second World War. For many Jews, this in itself is enough to negate cremation as a choice.

From the perspective of the needs of the mourners, cremation negates the possibilities of many Jewish rituals of mourning and memorializing, such as the burial service itself, the placing of a headstone and having a place to visit for surviving family. Cremation may not provide the sense of closure that a burial often does.

In a pluralistic Jewish community, however, some Jews will choose cremation over burial. Some raise concerns about cemeteries in terms of environmental issues and the use of scarce natural resources. Others may cite concerns about the costs associated with burial in contrast to cremation (although it is important to contrast the actual costs for a traditional Jewish burial that would avoid extravagance and unnecessary additions, such as flowers). Some choose cremation for spiritual or religious reasons as they understand them.

It is important for the family members to discuss such choices early on. Confronting cremation directives after death can cause conflict and heartache for the family if there is disagreement. A conflict of values may arise. An adult child opposed to cremation may wonder how to respect a parent's decision for cremation. Siblings or spouses may disagree about whether to support a decision for cremation.

Families in which an individual is considering cremation should discuss and attempt to resolve any differences well in advance of being confronted with the actual death. Adult children often feel obligated to honor the wishes of their parent/s even if the directives they leave indicate practices contrary to Jewish tradition and/or the comfort of the children. In navigating this sensitive area, some people will decide that the *mitzva* of *kibud av v'em*/honoring one's parents is determinative. Others will note that Judaism does not require children to carry out directives that are contrary to Jewish law, even if that was the desire of their parent/s. Different families may arrive at different decisions. Whatever decision is reached, families should strive to maintain *k'vod hamet*/respect for the deceased.

It is important to consult with one's rabbi to ascertain her/his position on cremation and officiation at memorial services, and to identify policies and customs of the local community. Rabbis can also clarify issues and help families discuss the issues they need to resolve.

When there is to be a cremation, it is recommended that a funeral service be conducted prior to the disposition of the body rather than holding a memorial service following the cremation. Local customs vary, but in many Jewish cemeteries, remains may be buried.

D. Jewish Holidays and Shiva

According to Jewish law, Shiva is ended regardless of how many days have been observed when a minimum of one hour has been observed before one of the major holidays begins. These include Rosh Hashana and Yom Kippur, Pesaḥ, Sukkot and Shavuot.

When a death and burial occur after a holiday has commenced but while it is still being observed (for example, the third day of Pesaḥ), the beginning of Shiva is supposed to be delayed until after the holiday concludes.

These practices suggest that the observances shared by all Jews (holidays) supersede those that are restricted to some Jews (in this case, mourners). They also speak to a practical reality—namely, that those who might be expected to come as comforters would, in a traditional community, be involved in the observance of the holidays and would be unlikely to be available to provide the very support that mourners might need.

For many contemporary Jews, however, the inability to observe Shiva fully because of the intervention of a holiday is experienced as a lost opportunity. Unable to shift between the sadness of mourning and the celebration of

---

The tradition of adjusting or ending Shiva when a holiday begins may seem to disregard the personal needs of the mourner, but is necessary if there are to be meaningful communal holidays. If one follows the traditional expectation that Shiva concludes with the arrival of a holiday, one may still choose to stay home for additional days, receive guests and recite prayers. While some of the formal observances of Shiva may end when the holiday begins (covering the mirrors, or sitting on low benches, for example), a period of retreat from life's normal demands remains important when one has experienced a loss. — D.E.

the holiday, many Jews are left with an incomplete experience on both counts.

It is difficult to disregard traditional teachings. The Jewish holidays are powerful, and we feel the pull of community even in our moments of individual sorrow. Few Jews could imagine foregoing the Pesaḥ Seder or Kol Nidre night in order to observe Shiva. But it is also difficult to disregard the emotional realities of a family following a death.

It is advisable to consult with a rabbi about the appropriate accommodation of Shiva to holidays in light of personal, family and community circumstances, customs and values. From a Reconstructionist perspective, which balances the imperatives and precedents of tradition with contemporary needs, the following adaptations may be considered:

1. Death, funeral and Shiva before and up to the start of a holiday:
   » If Shiva is already being observed when Rosh Hashana, Yom Kippur or Shavuot begins, rather than cutting off the remainder of Shiva, the formal/public aspects of Shiva should cease (as on Shabbat) until the holiday is concluded. A full or modified continuation of Shiva observance might resume at that time, with the intervening holiday days being counted (as is Shabbat) as part of the seven days.
   » If Shiva is already being observed when Pesaḥ and Sukkot commence, public observances of Shiva should be suspended on the first and last

days (which are "full" holiday observances), but intermediate days *(ḥol ha-mo'ed) should* count toward the days of Shiva and may be observed as a full or modified continuation of Shiva.

2. Death, funeral and Shiva on or during a holiday:

» Funerals traditionally do not occur on full holiday days. A funeral may occur during intermediate days *(ḥol hamo'ed)* of Pesaḥ or Sukkot (as well as on Purim or any day of Hanukka). When that happens, rather than waiting until after Pesaḥ or Sukkot are completed, Shiva might begin from the burial and continue until the onset of the closing day of the holiday, when it would either conclude or be temporarily suspended until the holiday ends, depending on the counting of Shiva days.

» Festivals also affect the counting of the thirty days for *sheloshim,* with the general tendency being for the onset of holidays to abridge or conclude the *sheloshim,* even if thirty days have not elapsed. Since the function of *sheloshim* is to carry mourners through the first month of the loss, it is suggested that *sheloshim* be counted as thirty days from the funeral regardless of the intervention of holidays.

E. Infant Death

In traditional Jewish law, the full requirements of mourning apply only when the deceased has lived beyond thirty days. While from a contemporary perspective this may appear harsh, in pre-modern times, when small communities had a high incidence of infant mortality, this was intended to be a compassionate gesture that would relieve individuals and the community from what would have been an almost continuous cycle of Shiva and mourning.

Today, however, it is important to affirm that (with the agreement of the family) in the tragic case of an infant death, the rituals of Jewish mourning should be offered to the family so that, in consultation with a rabbi, the family members can select the observances that would be comforting. While mourning a life of but a few hours, days or weeks is different than mourning a life lived over a period of many years, the sense of loss and grief experienced by the family deserves both respect and response from the Jewish community and Jewish tradition.

F. Interfaith Issues

In view of the changing demography of the Jewish community, with increasing numbers of intermarried and conversionary families welcomed into congregations, questions arise regarding mourning practices. In view of the complex and highly personal nature of these issues as they

As a result of ultrasound and other technologies, a fetus can have a manifest presence in the emotional life of the parents. If the fetus dies, families may seek a ritual of closure and comfort. I have found it powerful to participate in the burial of a fetus after a stillbirth or a late miscarriage, and to grieve with the family. In these circumstances, I have observed the transformative quality of this healing ritual. — S.P.W.

occur in individual families, it is helpful to consult with a rabbi when making decisions about observances of mourning. While the evolution of community customs and norms in this area is still very much in process, the following guidelines reflect an emerging sense of how to respond sensitively to interfaith issues of Jewish rituals for mourning.

1. Mourning for Non-Jews:

The question of whether Jews are obligated to observe mourning practices for non-Jews has received consideration in traditional Jewish sources, primarily in the context of the obligations that converts to Judaism have to mourn the death of their (non-Jewish) parents (and by extension, other first-degree relatives). The majority of opinions indicate that while a convert to Judaism has no obligation to observe traditional Jewish mourning practices, including Kaddish, for her/his parents, the convert may certainly do so if s/he wishes. A minority perspective suggests that such observance might be mandatory rather than optional. It can be deduced from this reasoning that a Jewish spouse

Although converts have the same religious identity as those born Jewish, their passing will have an impact on family members who are not Jewish, including parents and siblings. A convert may have a spouse/partner and/or children who observe Jewish mourning practices, but questions, concerns and expectations may come from bereaved non-Jewish relatives as well. Areas where attitudes may differ among religions (for example, autopsy, timing of the funeral or choice of cemetery) should be discussed clearly and openly to avoid disagreements and misunderstandings. — B.R.P.

might not be obligated to observe traditional mourning practices for a non-Jewish partner, but would certainly not be prohibited from doing so.

The assumptions behind this reasoning are not necessarily shared by contemporary Jews. Whereas traditional Jewish law focused on the *religious identity of the deceased,* Reconstructionist Jews would more likely focus on the *emotional and spiritual needs of the surviving family members.* The resources of Jewish tradition should help Jews throughout the period of loss and mourning. When the non-Jewish spouse/partner in an interfaith marriage dies, it is entirely appropriate for the surviving Jewish spouse/partner to observe the rituals of mourning. For these reasons, Reconstructionist Judaism encourages converts to observe Jewish mourning practices for their non-Jewish relatives.

2. Non-Jews as Mourners:

When a non-Jewish spouse/partner experiences the death of a Jewish spouse, the circumstances can be more complex. The non-Jewish spouse/partner may want a high degree of involvement with Jewish ritual, or, conversely, may not want to be under the presumption of participating in specifically Jewish observances.

Early in my rabbinate, I created considerable animosity in a Jewish woman who wanted to say Kaddish for her non-Jewish father. I simply missed the point of her need to mourn as a Jew. I did make amends to her years later. But I learned an important lesson about empowering and encouraging Jews to grieve their loved ones Jewishly, even when those they have lost are not Jewish. — S.P.W.

The degree to which a non-Jew chooses to participate in Jewish rituals of mourning will vary. If the non-Jewish spouse/partner is an active and/or affirming member of another religious community, s/he presumably participates in the rituals and traditions of that faith community as they pertain to and help support mourners, and will look primarily to that community at a time of loss.

When the non-Jewish spouse/partner is not active in or affirming of another religious tradition, the synagogue may, in fact, be his/her sole religious community, notwithstanding that s/he has never converted to Judaism. A community should show support for this member as it would for any other member. There may be adaptations and/or modifications of Jewish mourning practices. For example, at a Shiva observance, there may or may not be a recitation of the Jewish evening prayers; if there is, the surviving spouse may or may not recite the Kaddish, but the Jewish members of the congregation present should do so as a way for the community to mourn the loss.

Non-Jews are not obligated to observe *mitzvot*. They need not take on specifically Jewish observances, such as *k'ria* and the Kaddish. However, consider the example of a family with a Jewish father, non-Jewish mother and Jewish children. If the husband dies and the children (and other Jewish family members) are observing rituals of mourning while the wife is not, she would perhaps rightly feel excluded at a significant emotional moment in the life of the family. From that perspective, wearing a torn garment or a *k'ria* ribbon and joining the recitation of the Kaddish might be appropriate.

In general, non-Jews in Reconstructionist communities would be encouraged to share in the rituals of mourning that are in the realm of custom (as examples: placing earth in a grave, washing one's hands upon returning from the cemetery, sitting on low stools during Shiva) while considering the appropriateness of sharing rituals that specifically presume Jewish identity (as examples: reciting the Kaddish or the benediction for the *k'ria*).

I once officiated at the burial of a single woman who had converted to Judaism, whose Episcopalian relatives and friends deeply appreciated being able to participate in the *k'vura* (burial). — B.R.P.

For Everything there is a Season

The Bible teaches:

> For everything there is a season, a time for every
> experience under heaven:
> A time to be born and a time to die; a time to weep
> and a time to laugh;
> A time to grieve and a time to dance; a time to seek
> and a time to lose;
> A time to keep and a time to let go; a time to tear
> and a time to mend. (Ecclesiastes, chapter 3)

Each generation, given the gift of life by those who came
before, must eventually confront the loss of life. Mortality
is the common condition of humanity, transcending religions, cultures and nations. Our human relationships give
us warmth, meaning, companionship and love. When
those relationships are severed by death, we are, appro-
priately and understandably, plunged into sadness,
despair and grief.

Before we can let go of those we have loved, we pause.
We pause in order to take note of a life that has come to
its end. We pause to acknowledge grief, and we pause
long enough to allow those who grieve to be surrounded
by those who love them. And we pause because whenever
parting comes, it comes too soon, and we do not want to
have to say goodbye.

We look for the strength to withstand the sadness of loss and for the courage to endure in the presence of death. We pray for the ability to give as well as to receive comfort in our moments of mourning. We search for light amid the darkness, striving to accept the blessing of life that death so often seeks to deny. Judaism celebrates life as a blessing and a gift, and occasions of loss can make us aware—as perhaps no other occasions can—of the need to cherish each moment of life that we are given.

As Jews, we face the common human moment of grieving as other Jews have faced it before us: strengthened by faith in a power beyond us that bestows life and redeems death, comforted by the symbols and traditions of our people and by the friends and family who sit with us and reassure us with their presence, and sustained by the meanings we forge in moments of loss that enable us to move through the journey of mourning and emerge again into life.

In our inevitable moments of loss, may we be granted the peace that comes with the passing of time and the sustaining power of love that never dies. And may we so lead our lives that when the time comes for others to memorialize us, they will do so with affection, respect and love.

For Further Reading . . .

There are many resources for further exploration of Jewish approaches to death and mourning, and many books on those subjects include bibliographies of additional publications.

A Time to Mourn, A Time to Comfort by Ron Wolfson (Jewish Lights, 1996) is both accessible and comprehensive. *Saying Kaddish: How to Comfort the Dying, Bury the Dead, and Mourn as a Jew* by Anita Diamant (Schocken 1998) is a valuable contemporary volume. The classic text by Maurice Lamm, *The Jewish Way in Death and Mourning* (Jonathan David publishers) remains an important resource if one makes allowances for his generally conservative position within an Orthodox framework. *Mourning and Mitzvah, A Guided Journal* by Anne Brenner (Jewish Lights, 1993) helps take a mourner through the year following a death with insightful suggestions.

Jewish tradition has had many perspectives on issues of death and afterlife. *Jewish Views of the Afterlife,* by Simcha Paull Raphael (Jason Aronson, 1994) provides a comprehensive overview. *The Death of Death: Resurrection & Immortality in Jewish Thought* by Neil Gillman (Jewish Lights, 1997) offers a valuable civilizational approach, tracing relevant issues from the biblical period to the contemporary era. *What Happens After I Die?* by Rifat Sonsino and Daniel B. Syme (UAHC Press, 1990) offers a survey of sources relating to such ideas as immortality and resurrection, as well as several theological essays.

Recommended books reflecting a more personal approach to issues of death and loss include: *When a Jew Dies: the Ethnography of a Bereaved Son* by Samuel Heilman (University of California Press, 2001); *Living a Year of Kaddish* by Ari Goldman (Schocken, 2003); *Mornings and Mourning: A Kaddish Journal* by E.M. Broner (Harpers San Franciso, 1994); and an anthology edited by Jack Riemer, *Jewish Insights on Death and Mourning* (Schocken, 1995). *Kaddish* by Leon Wieseltier (Knopf, 1998) combines detailed research into the traditions of the Kaddish with the author's reflections on his year of mourning following the death of his father.

The Kaddish Prayer

(including translation and transliteration)

KADDISH YATOM /THE MOURNERS' KADDISH

Reader: Let God's name be made great and holy in the world that was created as God willed. May God complete the holy realm in your own lifetime, in your days, and in the days of all the house of Israel, quickly and soon. And say: Amen.

Congregation: May God's great name be blessed, forever and as long as worlds endure.

Reader: May it be blessed, and praised, and glorified, and held in honor, viewed with awe, embellished, and revered; and may the blessed name of holiness be hailed, though it be higher (*Between Rosh Hashanah and Yom Kippur, add:* by far) than all the blessings, songs, praises, and consolations that we utter in this world. And say: Amen.

May Heaven grant a universal peace, and life for us, and for all Israel. And say: Amen.

May the one who creates harmony above, make peace for us and for all Israel, and for all who dwell on earth. And say: Amen.

KADDISH YATOM /THE MOURNERS' KADDISH

קַדִּישׁ יָתוֹם

יִתְגַּדַּל וְיִתְקַדַּשׁ שְׁמֵהּ רַבָּא בְּעָלְמָא דִּי בְרָא כִרְעוּתֵהּ וְיַמְלִיךְ
מַלְכוּתֵהּ בְּחַיֵּיכוֹן וּבְיוֹמֵיכוֹן וּבְחַיֵּי דְכָל בֵּית יִשְׂרָאֵל בַּעֲגָלָא וּבִזְמַן
קָרִיב וְאִמְרוּ אָמֵן:

יְהֵא שְׁמֵהּ רַבָּא מְבָרַךְ לְעָלַם וּלְעָלְמֵי עָלְמַיָּא:

יִתְבָּרַךְ וְיִשְׁתַּבַּח וְיִתְפָּאַר וְיִתְרוֹמַם וְיִתְנַשֵּׂא וְיִתְהַדָּר וְיִתְעַלֶּה
וְיִתְהַלָּל שְׁמֵהּ דְּקֻדְשָׁא בְּרִיךְ הוּא

מִן כָּל בִּרְכָתָא (Between Rosh Hashanah and Yom Kippur, add: לְעֵלָּא) לְעֵלָּא
וְשִׁירָתָא תֻּשְׁבְּחָתָא וְנֶחֱמָתָא דַּאֲמִירָן בְּעָלְמָא וְאִמְרוּ אָמֵן:
יְהֵא שְׁלָמָא רַבָּא מִן שְׁמַיָּא וְחַיִּים עָלֵינוּ וְעַל כָּל יִשְׂרָאֵל וְאִמְרוּ אָמֵן:
עֹשֶׂה שָׁלוֹם בִּמְרוֹמָיו הוּא יַעֲשֶׂה שָׁלוֹם עָלֵינוּ וְעַל כָּל יִשְׂרָאֵל וְעַל
כָּל יוֹשְׁבֵי תֵבֵל וְאִמְרוּ אָמֵן:

Reader: Yitgadal veyitkadash shemey raba
be'alma di vera ḥirutey veyamliḥ malḥutey
behayeyhon uvyomeyhon uvḥayey deḥol beyt yisra'el
ba'agala uvizman kariv ve'imru amen.

Congregation: Yehey shemey raba mevaraḥ le'alam ulalmey almaya.

Reader: Yitbaraḥ veyishtabaḥ veyitpa'ar veyitromam veyitnasey
veyit-hadar veyitaleh veyit-halal shemey dekudsha beriḥ hu
le'ela (*Between Rosh Hashanah and Yom Kippur, add:* le'ela) min kol birhata
veshirata tushbeḥata veneḥemata da'amiran be'alma ve'imru
amen.

Yehey shelama raba min shemaya veḥayim <u>aleynu</u> ve'al kol
yisra'el ve'imru amen.

Oseh shalom bimromav hu ya'aseh shalom <u>aleynu</u> ve'al kol
yisra'el ve'al kol yoshvey tevel ve'imru amen.

Conclusion of Shiva

To be read by the mourner(s) on the morning of the conclusion of Shiva.

As Jewish tradition prescribes Shiva, a period of intense mourning, so too does it prescribe a moment when Shiva ends. Today, we walk out the door of the Shiva house back into engagement with daily concerns. Mourning is far from over, but today we take important steps back into life. At this moment, we ask:

יהוה עֹז לְעַמּוֹ יִתֵּן יהוה יְבָרֵךְ אֶת־עַמּוֹ בַשָּׁלוֹם:

Adonay oz le'amo yiten, adonay yivareḥ et amo vashalom.

May You, REDEEMING ONE, give strength to your people. May You, ETERNAL ONE, bless your people with peace.

MERCIFUL ONE, grant healing, comfort, and strength to those who mourn the loss of _____ . May his/her memory be a source of blessing in their lives. May they find consolation and peace with each other and return to doing deeds that strengthen the bonds of the living. Amen.

יהוה נְחֵנִי בְצִדְקָתֶךָ הַיְשַׁר לְפָנַי דַּרְכֶּךָ:

Adonay neḥeni vetzidkateḥa hayeshar lefanay darkeḥa.

GUIDING ONE, lead me in your righteousness, make your path straight before me.

May I take to heart the love and lessons of the life of _____ and of this Shiva as I walk again into life.

It is customary to walk a short distance. Some people circle the block on which they live.

יהוה עֹז...בשלום / May...peace! (Psalms 29:11).

יהוה...דרכך / Guiding...me. (Psalms 5:9).

A Service for Dedication
for a Memorial Marker or Headstone
(Unveiling)

There is little formal liturgy associated with dedications. It is customary to include the memorial prayer El Maley Raḥamim *("God full of compassion") in Hebrew and/or English and the Kaddish. Since headstone dedications are in the realm of custom and not law, psalms, readings, poems and/or family reflections can be shared as well. Dedications can normally be handled by a family without having a rabbi present, although families may want to consult with a rabbi before the ceremony itself.*

In some communities, the custom is to cover the marker or headstone at the beginning of the ceremony. Any clean cloth or covering can be used.

Opening Prayer

We gather today to honor the memory of _____. As we think of (him/her), we are reminded of the bonds of love and caring and the bonds of family and friendship that sustain us in our moments of loss.

We turn to the words of the Psalms for wisdom and perspective:

> O God, what are we, that you have regard for us?
> What are we, that you take notice of us?
> We are like a breath; our days are like a passing shadow;
> we are like the grass, which in the morning sprouts
>   renewed,
> and in the evening withers and fades.

We return to the earth, as you remind us to return to You;
If only we could comprehend, and understand our destiny;
For when we die, we carry nothing away;
our accomplishments will not sustain us.

The span of our life is seventy years,
given the strength, perhaps eighty years;
They pass so quickly, and we are in darkness.
Teach us, therefore, to number our days wisely.

Turn to us, O God, and may Your presence be with us.
You have been our shelter in every generation.
Before the mountains came into being,
before You brought forth the earth and the world,
from eternity to eternity You are God.

And so we lift our eyes to the mountains;
what is the source of our help?
Our help comes from God, the Maker of heaven and earth.
So may God guard our souls now and forever.

(Adapted from various psalms)

A Time for Memories

In Jewish tradition, we add the words "May (his/her) memory be a blessing" to the name of those whose journey in this world has come to an end. Some memories come in an overpowering rush; others drift into our consciousness more gradually. Sometimes, it is the little things that surface over time that turn out to be the most precious and important. This is a time for memory.

(David A. Teutsch, adapted)

At this point, people can be invited to share a thought, a memory or a prayer from the heart. A few minutes of quiet reflection are also appropriate.

Dedication

Rabbi Shimon taught: There are three crowns: the crown of Torah, the crown of the ancient Temple priesthood, and the crown of royal power. But the "Crown of the Good Name"—the *Keter Shem Tov*—surpasses them all.

As today we remember _____, we dedicate this marker in (his/her) memory. We pray that the name here sanctified will be a source of blessing for the living, and will be remembered in the generations to come.

If a covering has been used, it is now removed

Choose one of the following, or another reading, prayer or poem that seems appropriate.

From "Dirge Without Music"
by Edna St. Vincent Millay

I am not resigned to the shutting away of loving hearts in
    the hard ground.
So it is, and so it will be, for so it has been, time out of
    mind:
Into the darkness they go, the wise and the lovely.
Crowned with lilies and with laurel they go; but I am not
    resigned.

Down, down, down into the darkness of the grave
Gently they go, the beautiful, the tender, the kind;
Quietly they go, the intelligent, the witty, the brave.
I know. But I do not approve. And I am not resigned.

Psalm 23

The Eternal is my shepherd; I shall never be in need.
Amid the choicest grasses does God set me down.
God leads me by the calmest waters, and restores my soul.
God takes me along paths of righteousness,
In keeping with the honor of God's name.

Even should I wander in a valley of the darkest shadows,
I will fear no evil.
You are with me, God. Your power and support
   are there to comfort me.
You set in front of me a table
in the presence of my enemies.
You anoint my head with oil; my cup is overflowing.
Surely, good and loving-kindness will pursue me
   all the days of my life,
And I shall come to dwell inside the house
   of the Eternal for a length of days.

At this point, the El Maley Raḥamim *prayer can be recited in Hebrew and/or English; the text can be found on pages 79–80. If the Hebrew/Jewish name of the deceased is unknown, the word "y'kareynu" ("our beloved one") can be inserted at the appropriate place. This can be followed by the Kaddish, found on pages 72–73.*

Closing Reflection

It is customary to place small stones on a memorial marker before we leave. Our ancestors wisely used this symbolic act to help transform sadness and sorrow into an honoring of the enduring qualities of those they loved.

As we preserve the name and memory of _____, so we preserve (his/her) accomplishments; we dedicate ourselves to the causes and concerns (he/she) supported; we link our lives to (his/hers) and affirm that what is precious and vital in human life endures in the life of eternity.

Amen.

A Ritual for Yahrtzeit Licht/
Lighting a Memorial Candle

A yahrtzeit candle is lit on the anniversary of the death of a loved one and before lighting festival candles the evening before Yizkor is recited.

These prayers are also said when visiting a grave; however, in that case the yahrtzeit candle is omitted.

Merciful God, I turn to you in prayer at this time of remembrance. The link of life that bound me to _____ has been broken, but feelings of love continue to bind us together. I give thanks for the gift of _____'s life, companionship, and memory. Help me understand how my life has been formed and shaped by what _____ was and did. I pray for the strength to live by the light of the highest ideals we shared.

The yahrtzeit candle is now lit.

זִכְרוֹנוֹ/זִכְרוֹנָהּ לִבְרָכָה:

Zikhrono livrakha/zikhrona livrakha.

May his/her memory be a blessing.

As long as we live, they too will live.
for they are part of us
as long as we remember them.

For a man or boy:

אֵל מָלֵא רַחֲמִים שׁוֹכֵן בַּמְּרוֹמִים הַמְצֵא מְנוּחָה נְכוֹנָה תַּחַת כַּנְפֵי הַשְּׁכִינָה בְּמַעֲלוֹת קְדוֹשִׁים וּטְהוֹרִים כְּזֹהַר הָרָקִיעַ מַזְהִירִים אֶת נִשְׁמַת _____ : בַּעַל הָרַחֲמִים יַסְתִּירֵהוּ בְּסֵתֶר כְּנָפָיו לְעוֹלָמִים וְיִצְרוֹר בִּצְרוֹר הַחַיִּים אֶת נִשְׁמָתוֹ: יהוה הוּא נַחֲלָתוֹ וְיָנוּחַ עַל מִשְׁכָּבוֹ בְּשָׁלוֹם וְנֹאמַר אָמֵן:

אֵל מָלֵא רַחֲמִים שׁוֹכֵן בַּמְּרוֹמִים הַמְצֵא מְנוּחָה נְכוֹנָה תַּחַת כַּנְפֵי
הַשְּׁכִינָה בְּמַעֲלוֹת קְדוֹשִׁים וּטְהוֹרִים כְּזֹהַר הָרָקִיעַ מַזְהִירִים אֶת
נִשְׁמַת _____ : בַּעַל הָרַחֲמִים יַסְתִּירָהָ בְּסֵתֶר כְּנָפָיו
לְעוֹלָמִים וְיִצְרוֹר בִּצְרוֹר הַחַיִּים אֶת נִשְׁמָתָהּ: יהוה הוּא נַחֲלָתָהּ
וְתָנוּחַ עַל מִשְׁכָּבָהּ בְּשָׁלוֹם וְנֹאמַר אָמֵן:

God full of mercy who dwells in high places, grant full repose
under *Shekhina's* wings in the heights of the holy and
pure—like a light glowing in the firmament—to the soul of
_____ . Merciful one, conceal him/her under your
wings forever, and bind his/her soul to life. THE
COMPASSIONATE is his/her portion. May he/she rest in peace in
his/her place. Amen.

A Ritual for Closing a Home Following a Death

BY RICHARD HIRSH

Shortly after the death of my mother, I found myself in her apartment, facing the task of emptying out and closing up a home. As anyone who has had to face this experience can attest, this task brings with it a wide range of demands, physical as well as emotional.

After many phone calls, all the necessary arrangements were made. The things we decided to keep were packed and mailed back home. The things we gave away went to various charities and thrift shops. What remained was simply thrown away. And when the apartment itself was finally empty, it was time to lock up, hand in the keys and leave, knowing that we would not be back.

It was at that moment that I realized that there was no ritual way to mark this event, and particularly this moment of this event. I had been (understandably) so busy with all the arrangements for which I was responsible that I had not anticipated the need to structure ritually this transitional moment.

I further realized that even if I had anticipated that need, there was no obvious place to look in the catalogue of Jewish traditions and rituals. There are many variations on the ceremony of *ḥanukat habayit* (dedication of a home)—many of which are amplified versions of the blessing and ritual for affixing a *mezuza*—but there is no parallel ritual for ending the connection to a home.

In thinking about what one might do by way of closing a home following the death of a parent, I am aware that people and their parents have differing relationships. Some are wonderful, some are terrible, many are somewhere in between—and all of them are complex. Some might find closing a home a sad but also comforting moment; others might experience it as both sad and saddening—calling up too many difficult moments of a difficult relationship. In the suggestions that follow, I have tried to account for this range of reactions with some alternatives in the suggested ritual.

1. Upon entering the home, one might recite Ma Tovu:

מַה טֹּבוּ אֹהָלֶיךָ יַעֲקֹב מִשְׁכְּנֹתֶיךָ יִשְׂרָאֵל

Ma tovu ohalekha Ya'akov, mishkenotekha Yisra'el

How good are your residences, O Jacob; your dwelling places, O Israel.

2. Consider placing a photograph of the deceased in a central place and kindling a *yahrtzeit* candle alongside it, making the presence of the deceased tangible.

3. Decisions have to be made about what to keep. Begin by acknowledging that the living have no way of knowing the value and meaning that the deceased attached to each object in the home, and that inevitably something that ought to have been kept will be given away and pass out of the family. We pray to act as the deceased would have wanted, and we ask forgiveness in advance for any inadvertent transgressions.

4. In cleaning out a home, we inevitably come across certain things for which we have no use, yet with which we cannot part. Perhaps we only want them preserved for children and grandchildren, recognizing how few objects actually survive the march of the generations. Stories, memories and customs are often passed down; how many people can hold in their hands actual objects that their grandparents and great grandparents held, used, displayed in their homes?

   Designate one or more boxes as a *geniza*. A *geniza* is where Jewish tradition directs us to place worn ritual objects as well as any piece of paper bearing the four letter Hebrew name of God. Items that are holy are saved for sacred storage and/or eventual burial.

   "What are we going to do with that?" is the often-asked question when closing a home. Sometimes, the answer only needs to be "keep it." Having a *geniza* helps us set aside objects whose sanctity lies simply in their having been a part of our family and its story.

5. Acts of generosity in the name of the deceased are central to Jewish tradition. Determine what can be donated to charity as an act of *tzedaka* on behalf of one who can no longer contribute her/himself.

6. The most difficult moment in closing a home comes when "the work" is done, when the now-empty home stands in silent evocation of the absence of the person who once lived there, and who was a part of our lives. What might be done by way of ritual expression before one crosses the threshold and turns the key for the last time?

A prayer that might be brought forward at this moment is a brief prayer adapted from the confessional of the Yom Kippur service ("*Al Ḥet*," "for the sin we have sinned by. . . ."). Even in the best of relationships, a large part of the grieving process is making peace with the memory of the deceased. Especially when dealing with a parent, the complex and complicated weave of history, feeling and fact rarely leaves any of us without some ambiguity and some unresolved issues.

Reciting the confession of sin in the now-empty home of our parent/s is a way of acknowledging the pain we no doubt caused, even if inadvertent; the offenses, both conscious and unintentional, that we visited upon our parents; and of asking for their forgiveness. It is also a moment in which to acknowledge the pain parents may have caused us, the offenses both intended and inadvertent, the hurts and the wounds—and to offer our forgiveness.

A Short Prayer of Confession and Reconciliation

For the wrong that we may have done whether by
    intention or by mistake;
For the wrong that we may have done in the
    closing of the heart;
For the wrong that we may have done through
    judgment or condescension;
For the wrong that we may have done by
    unwillingness to change;
For the wrong that we may have done by
    condemning in our parents the faults we
    tolerate in ourselves;
For the wrong that we may have done by
    withholding love;
For the wrong that we may have done by not
    accepting love;
For the wrong that we may have done by
    pretending not to hear;

For the wrong that we may have done by choosing
     not to make the time that we should have;
For the wrong that we may have done by waiting
     too long to say what we should have said;
For the wrong that we may have done by
     dismissing wisdom;
For the wrong that we may have done by
     refusing to compromise;
For the wrong that we may have done by
     devaluing what others honored;
For the wrong that we may have done by empty
     promises;
For the wrong that we may have done through
     confusion of the heart;
For the wrong that we may have done by
     withholding honor that was earned;
May we start to let go of whatever pain and
     disappointment lingers;
find the compassion to forgive, and the courage
     to be forgiven;
in the blessing of memory, may we find a place
     for peace.

7. Following the recitation of this *Al Ḥet* and the asking
   and offering of forgiveness, additional readings, biblical passages, or poetry might be recited, as appropriate.
   Here, family traditions should be included. A favorite
   or meaningful passage from the life of the family in the
   home can speak as strongly as an "official prayer."

   A suggested text is adapted from the biblical book of
   Proverbs, chapter four:

   Children, heed the discipline of a parent;
   Listen and learn discernment,
   For I gave you good instruction;
   Do not forsake my teaching.

   Once I was a son to my father,
   The tender beloved of my mother.
   They instructed me and said to me,

   Let your mind hold on to my words;
   Keep my teachings and you will live.
   Acquire wisdom, acquire discernment;
   Do not forget my words.

My children, listen to what I have said;
Incline your ear to recall my words.
Do not lose sight of them;
Keep them in your mind.

8. It is time for the removal of the *mezuza* on the main
doorway (and/or *mezuzot* on the other doorways of the
home). As the affixing of a *mezuza* at the beginning of
one's residence in a home is a symbol of consecration
and identification, removing it is a necessary symbol
confronting the reality that we can no longer identify
this home with this person.

There is a custom of leaving a *mezuza* in place
so that if the next resident of a house is Jewish and
either neglects to attach a *mezuza* or does not do so in
a timely manner, the house will not be lacking this symbol. If one is concerned about maintaining this tradition, consider leaving a new *mezuza* inside the home
with an appropriate note explaining (if the new resident
is Jewish) what it is and how it is attached, and also
leave (in the case where the new resident is not Jewish)
a pre-paid mailer addressed to the nearest synagogue
with a note to give the *mezuza* to someone who needs
one.

9. Recite the *El Maley Raḥamim* prayer in which we pray
that the deceased be gathered under the wings of the
Shekhina and be bound up in the bond of life:

For a man or boy:

אֵל מָלֵא רַחֲמִים שׁוֹכֵן בַּמְּרוֹמִים הַמְצֵא מְנוּחָה נְכוֹנָה תַּחַת כַּנְפֵי
הַשְּׁכִינָה בְּמַעֲלוֹת קְדוֹשִׁים וּטְהוֹרִים כְּזֹהַר הָרָקִיעַ מַזְהִירִים אֶת
נִשְׁמַת _____ : בַּעַל הָרַחֲמִים יַסְתִּירֵהוּ בְּסֵתֶר כְּנָפָיו
לְעוֹלָמִים וְיִצְרוֹר בִּצְרוֹר הַחַיִּים אֶת נִשְׁמָתוֹ: יהוה הוּא נַחֲלָתוֹ
וְיָנוּחַ עַל מִשְׁכָּבוֹ בְּשָׁלוֹם וְנֹאמַר אָמֵן:

For a woman or girl:

אֵל מָלֵא רַחֲמִים שׁוֹכֵן בַּמְּרוֹמִים הַמְצֵא מְנוּחָה נְכוֹנָה תַּחַת כַּנְפֵי
הַשְּׁכִינָה בְּמַעֲלוֹת קְדוֹשִׁים וּטְהוֹרִים כְּזֹהַר הָרָקִיעַ מַזְהִירִים אֶת
נִשְׁמַת _____ : בַּעַל הָרַחֲמִים יַסְתִּירָהּ בְּסֵתֶר כְּנָפָיו
לְעוֹלָמִים וְיִצְרוֹר בִּצְרוֹר הַחַיִּים אֶת נִשְׁמָתָהּ: יהוה הוּא נַחֲלָתָהּ
וְתָנוּחַ עַל מִשְׁכָּבָהּ בְּשָׁלוֹם וְנֹאמַר אָמֵן:

Merciful God of compassion, dwelling in the heights of heaven, grant complete rest in your protective presence along with those holy and pure, whose radiance is like that of the firmament, to the soul of _____. Compassionate God, gather (him/her) to you forever, that (his/her) soul may be bound up in the bond of life; through you we are granted a share of eternity. May (he/she) rest in peace. Amen.

10. Extinguish the *yahrtzeit* candle that has burned throughout the closing of the home. Take the picture that has stood alongside it. Words from tradition that might be spoken at this moment:

בָּרוּךְ אַתָּה יהוה אֱלֹהֵינוּ מֶלֶךְ הָעוֹלָם דַּיַּן הָאֱמֶת

Barukh Ata Adonay Eloheynu Melekh Ha'olam, Dayan Ha'emet: Praised is the Judge of truth (the traditional words acknowledging loss).

בָּרוּךְ אַתָּה יהוה אֱלֹהֵינוּ מֶלֶךְ הָעוֹלָם הַטּוֹב וְהַמֵּטִיב

Barukh Ata Adonay Eloheynu Melekh Ha'olam, Hatov V'ha-metiv: Praised is the One, life of all existence, who essence is the goodness we experience (the benediction of appreciation for the good things we have experienced).

יהוה יִשְׁמָר־צֵאתְךָ וּבוֹאֶךָ מֵעַתָּה וְעַד־עוֹלָם

Adonay yishmar tzeytekha u'vo'ekha, me'ata v'ad olam: May God watch over you when you go out and when you come in, now and always.

And then, we close the door for the last time.

Biographies of Contributors

DANIEL GOLDMAN CEDARBAUM is the president of the Jewish Reconstructionist Federation, a member of the Jewish Reconstructionist Congregation in Evanston, Illinois, and an attorney in private practice.

RABBI DAN EHRENKRANTZ is president of the Reconstructionist Rabbinical College and its Aaron & Marjorie Ziegelman presidential professor. A past president of the Reconstructionist Rabbinical Association, he previously was rabbi of Congregation Bnai Keshet in Montclair, New Jersey.

RABBI DAYLE A. FRIEDMAN directs Hiddur: The Center for Aging and Judaism of the Reconstructionist Rabbinical College. She is the editor of *Jewish Pastoral Care: A Practical Handbook from Traditional and Contemporary Sources* (Jewish Lights, 2001).

RABBI RICHARD HIRSH is Executive Director of the Reconstructionist Rabbinical Association and Editor of *The Reconstructionist* journal. He teaches at the Reconstructionist Rabbinical College.

RABBI MYRIAM KLOTZ teaches Torah, yoga and Jewish spirituality, leads retreats, and works in a variety of settings. She is on the staff of the Institute for Jewish Spirituality and on the faculty of Yedidya: Center for Jewish Spiritual Direction.

RABBI BARBARA ROSMAN PENZNER is the rabbi of Temple Hillel B'nai Torah in West Roxbury, Massachusetts and a past president of the Reconstructionist Rabbinical Association.

RABBI LINDA POTEMKEN is the rabbi of Congregation Beth Israel in Media, Pennsylvania. She teaches at the Reconstructionist Rabbinical College and has served as a teacher, consultant, therapist, and chaplain in a variety of settings.

DR. SIMCHA RAPHAEL teaches in the Department of Religion at La Salle University in Philadelphia and serves as a Spiritual Director at the Reconstructionist Rabbinical College. He also works as a psychotherapist, and is the author of *Jewish Views of the Afterlife* (Jason Aaronson, 1994).

RABBI YAEL RIDBERG is the rabbi of West End Synagogue in New York City. She was the first Marshall T. Meyer Rabbinic Fellow at Congregation B'nai Jeshurun in New York.

RABBI BRANT ROSEN is the rabbi of the Jewish Reconstructionist Congregation in Evanston, Illinois, and president of the Reconstructionist Rabbinical Association.

RABBI SHEILA PELTZ WEINBERG is Outreach Director and a staff member teaching meditation at the Institute for Jewish Spirituality. She has previously served as a congregational rabbi, Hillel director and community relations professional.

DAVID ZINNER is the Executive Director of *Kavod v'Nichum*, a resource center for Jewish burial societies in North America, and vice president of the Jewish Funeral Practices Committee of Greater Washington.

Index